the
SENIORS'
GUIDE
to life
in the slow lane

the
SENIORS'
GUIDE
to life
in the slow lane

Edited by
Pamela Chichinskas and Lynette Stokes

Eden Press
Montréal

THE SENIORS' GUIDE TO LIFE IN THE SLOW LANE
Edited by Pamela Chichinskas & Lynette Stokes

ISBN: 0-920792-63-4

Original cover cartoon: Tony Jenkins
Cover design: Luba Zagurak with Pamela Chichinskas and Lynette Stokes
Inside book design and illustrations: Lynette Stokes
Photo credits: Photographs are from the private collections of D. Chichinskas, C. Johnson, and M. Barton
Inside cartoons by Graham Harrop
The editors would like to thank the hundreds of Seniors who completed our questionnaires used to complete the "Top Ten Lists" in this book.

Printed in Canada at Metropole Litho Inc.
Dépot légal — première trimestre 1986
Bibliothèque nationale du Québec

Eden Press
4626 St.Catherine Street W.
Montreal Quebec
Canada H3Z 1S3

Main entry under title:
    The Seniors' guide to life in the slow lane

ISBN 0-920792-63-4

1. Old age--Anecdotes, facetiae, satire, etc.
I. Chichinskas, Pamela II. Stokes, Lynette

PN   6231.A43G64   1986   C86-090052-5
                                 C814'.54'083520565

The oldest hath borne most: we that are young,
Shall never see so much, nor live so long.

King Lear
V.iii.325-6

For Michael and Doreen Chichinskas, Violet O'Brien,
Leslie and Beatrice Stokes,
and all other parents whose children thought they knew better.

About Our Authors

Marie Barton was born in Denmark in 1905. She taught school in Saskatchewan at the age of eighteen, and was widowed with four dependents at thirty-eight. She obtained her B.A. and B.Ed. when she was fifty-one, and had her first published byline at the age of fourteen and her next at sixty-eight. She says it's been fun.

Mark Brown is the supervising psychologist for the Geriatric Treatment Unit of Connecticut Valley Hospital. Born in Plant City, Florida, he received his training in Florida, Idaho and California. While taking his work with Seniors seriously, he values humour for the perspective it provides.

Patrick Cotter is currently experimenting with an early working retirement in Florida with his wife, year-old son, and five unemployed cats.

Audrey Grayson is assistant Archivist and Leadership consultant for the Federation of Women Teachers Association of Ontario. She has always been a designer, at play in childhood, and professionally in adulthood. She is sixty-four years old, married, and has two successful daughters.

Tony Jenkins is an editorial cartoonist for the *Globe and Mail* and author of *Traveller's Tales: An Illustrated Journey Through Australia, Asia and Africa.* He is currently on sabbatical and touring South America.

Catherine B. (Webster) Jensen, generally known as Renée, was born in 1914 in Vancouver, B.C. Graduating from the Vancouver General Hospital School of Nursing in 1937, Renée married in 1940 and is blessed with two sons. Widowed just a year ago, two lively grandsons keep her in touch with the younger generation. She also writes a column for and about Seniors in *The West Ender.*

Fred Kerner, a Montreal-born Torontonian, is honorably retired. He is Editor Emeritus of Harlequin Books, but finds it hard to be a dotard. He spends his time word-watching, writing, and acting as a consultant to the publishing industry — and others who foolishly think publishing can be profitable.

Leonard L. Knott has been newspaperman, editor, author, public relations consultant and lecturer. Now in his eighties, his latest contributions to literature are *Writing for the Joy of It,* and *Writing After Fifty,* published by Writer's Digest Books.

Robert Ludwig has his background as a newsman, and served with the Canadian Forces as a Political Intelligence operator in Europe during WWII. He is now retired from his own business, Industrial Survey Services. He produces an infrequent column on subjects of concern to Seniors. He is seventy-seven.

Dorothy C. Lynch lives and loves in Winnipeg. On retirement, she decided to write because a pencil and paper are easier to carry around than a harp. She writes principally for *Seniors Today,* which is the only weekly newspaper in Canada of its kind, using the pseudonym " Augusta Wind."

Blaine McTavish, a Montreal free-lance writer, has written extensively on sports and mental health. Her travel articles are widely read. She has mixed feelings about her future as a Senior Citizen.

Leif Montin was born in Edinburgh in 1901, and emmigrated to Canada in time to witness the Halifax explosion of 1917. He is now retired and lives in Montreal. He has had a life-long love affair with cars.

John Moriarty and Ann Nazzaro met each other and soon realized that marriage and old age were inevitable. The two of them live in North Hampton, Massachusetts with a cat named Loretta.

Eric Nicol was born in Kingston, Ontario in 1919, and spent most of his working life as a syndicated humour columnist for *The Province,* in Vancouver, B.C., where he makes his home. A three-time winner of the Leacock Medal, he also writes stage, TV and radio plays.

Nicholas Pashley was born in Sussex, England, in 1887. He danced with Mata Hari at Maxim's in 1912, fled Petrograd through a misunderstanding in 1927, won 100 francs from Hemingway at croquet in 1928, appeared as a Munchkin in *The Wizard of Oz*, and introduced Jack Kennedy to Marilyn Monroe. A born liar, he now lives in Canada as a free-lance writer.

Jack Peach was born in Calgary, where he has lived and worked for fifty-five years. He also worked for seventeen years in Vancouver, London (England), Montreal, Ottawa and Edmonton. He has written and voiced eight hundred historical vignettes for CBC radio, and regularly contributed to *The Calgary Herald*. He has published three books.

George Wilson Powell, from Ste-Agathe, Quebec, had a checkered career after WWII service. He's been a broadcaster, public relations man, hotelier, and federal public servant. The high point of a low-key life was in 1962 when he became the first Canadian to fly over the Alps in a balloon, an event from which he has reportedly derived more mileage in after-dinner speeches than actually flown during the trip. Now retired, he strives to keep both feet firmly planted on the ground.

Frank B. Ricard, born in Sudbury, Ontario in 1915, worked for the Government of Quebec for twenty-eight years as a court stenographer. Now retired, he is a happy well-adjusted pensioner who's devoted to his delightful Irish wife Betty. As a *bon vivant*, he enjoys reading, playing the violin, gourmet cooking, and writing letters to the editor.

Claire Richardson was born in England, where she married her Canadian husband in 1946. She has been writing humourous articles and letters for many years, and is an opera lover and a prolific reader. The Richardsons live in London, Ontario, with their daughter Robin and grandson, Simon. Their son lives in Vancouver. Claire is seventy-two going on thirty-five. Age to her is simply a number.

Stuart Richardson is a likeable old codger and ancient mariner now long retired from the sea. He lives in a home with ten crabby old men and one hundred and fifteen lively ladies. He is the most popular man in the house and everyone speaks well of him.

Elizabeth Ruggier, a reluctant septagenarian, edits an international fur magazine, and is a free-lance writer and tireless world traveller. "The slow lane," she says, "is for centenarians."

G. Arthur Sage, author of *The Completely Civil Servant*, is a retired bureaucrat. Born in Saskatchewan, he earned academic accolades at the University of Toronto, Oxford and Harvard. He rose rapidly in the civil service and became known as a "deputy's deputy" because of his knack for handling just about any department. He is now enjoying a well-earned retirement in Vermont.

Les Stokes, born in Birmingham, England, now lives in North Wales. Having spent over thirty years in the construction business, he now prefers to write about home improvements than do any. He prefers watching cricket to either.

Jean Tansley is seventy-two years old and a member of the North York Seniors Centre.

Rae Thomas was born in rural Morden, Manitoba, in 1926. She was a Registered Nurse and is married with three daughters. After retirement, she began to write seriously, and has been published in Canada and the U.K. She is also a volunteer at the Hudson Bay Company archives.

Edna Willoughby is the retired co-publisher/owner of Saskatchewan's former weekly newspaper, *The Milestone Mail*. Born and educated in Milestone, near Regina, she married the local publisher and gradually became an interviewer, columnist, and news editor — as well as rearing a son and daughter. An ardent ragtime pianist, Edna entertains at Seniors' programs and enjoys a wealth of good friends and good books.

Table of Contents

INTRODUCTION

This is the first humour book written by Seniors, for Seniors, and about Seniors. But what's a *Senior*? According to the *Oxford Dictionary*, a Senior is "superior in age or standing to; of higher or highest degree." Well, that's not bad for a start, but it doesn't really do justice to a section of society whose ages and backgrounds are so diverse. However, there is one experience they all share; they are all discriminated against because of their ages.

These days, a sixty-fifth birthday arrives with a lot of unwanted baggage: mandatory retirement, loss of status, loss of income, and loss of power. Even so, travelling in the slow lane has rewards of its own. Seniors can stop and look at the scenery, and they see the people hurrying in the fast lane more clearly than those people see themselves.

We put this book together because we think everyone can benefit from this objectivity, and, judging from the overwhelming response to the project from across the continent, Seniors also think it's time they had their say.

A more enthusiastic group of writers can't be found; nor more professional, nor reliable, nor well-informed. Nor have we met a group with their tongues more firmly in their cheeks. In fact, our only complaint is that we simply didn't have enough space to accomodate more of their submissions.

So read on. Whether you're a Senior or a junior, you'll learn that there's more to life in the slow lane than retirement, support hose and bingo. There's a whole lot of living going on. After all, don't expect those who have lived through the Depression and WWII, as well as staggering political, technological and social changes, to take age discrimination lying down.

Pamela Chichinskas and Lynette Stokes
Montreal

ACKNOWLEDGEMENTS We would like to thank all of the Seniors' networks and organizations that referred an enormous number of talented writers to us. Specifically we would like to give a special thank you to Marie Barton, Professor of Creative Writing, Winnipeg; Heather Fraser of the New Horizons Program, Vancouver; Kay Stovold, President of the West End Seniors' Network, Vancouver; and the North York Seniors' Centre, Toronto. Plus all those Seniors for whose submissions we just didn't have the space. Lastly, we would like to thank Eden Press: Fawn Duchaine, Laura Foam, Sharon Thompson and Evelyne Hertel; and our Publisher, Sherri Clarkson, for making it all possible.

MILESTONE
SIXTY-FIVE

MILESTONE SIXTY-FIVE

by Dorothy C. Lynch

Milestone Sixty-Five won't be a millstone around my middle. No sirree! When the Birthday Man comes knocking on my door, I'll be ready. I've been anticipating his call for two years.

I've been conditioning myself for optimum action once he presents me with the hundreds of freebies and bonuses that I believe are my entitlement. I've been running up and down the basement stairs so I can leap nimbly onto a city bus, for twenty-five cents instead of eighty. I'm up to three miles per day in my walking program, shaping up for everything the future has to offer that is most enjoyable on foot; touring other cities and strolling along country lanes. I've managed to slice ten pounds off my tallish frame, so that calorie counting can be forgotten, should I find the time to travel and eat my way around the world — at a discount.

I'm back tasting the business world too, filling out applications and other forms in connection with my anticipated monthly goodies, like the old age pension and a transit pass.

As Fall approaches, I'm reading up on every program in the performing arts that the city has to offer me in my soon-to-be-acquired new status. The plethora of continuing education courses available at the university and government-funded agencies astounds me. They're reasonable and scheduled for daylight hours, when streets are safe. I can't possibly find enough time to do everything, but try to I surely will. Maybe, just maybe, there is a latent Picasso or a Margaret Mitchell lurking somewhere in my aging body, straining to get out.

At Christmas time, I'll flit around downtown, taking advantage of the special days on which I'll be entitled to buy dolls, candy canes, ties and slippers with discounted dollars. Great! Come income-tax filing time, I'll have exemptions here and exemptions there that I never had before. I know right now that I'll accept them with glee, for I've paid my dues and paid them well. They'll be my reward without waiting till I go to Heaven.

Springtime will turn the airport into my second home. I'll be in and out, travelling as often as I can — with a smile on my face. The discounts will make visiting places I've seen before appear rosier. In preparation, I've read the advice of the experts about travelling as healthfully as possible. Basically, it is to eat lightly, consume non-alcoholic drinks frequently and do isometric exercises while airborne.

My third home will be the bus depot. My magic, plastic picture card will work wonders. It will provide reasonable fares and a reduction in the price of accomodation and meals in many places along my freedom pathway. For instance, take such retirement havens as Florida and Arizona; there are freebies galore for we of the privileged class. Many restaurants offer full-course meals at give-away prices if you dine early and are a "mature" citizen.

Reduced airfares to Hawaii will land you in Paradise, where one known trick — staying longer than three weeks — will enable you to take free bus tours whenever you wish. The idea is to apply for a senior citizen's pass the day you arrive. You'll receive your permit about four weeks later. As the transit system — a modern one equipped with very comfortable seats as well as air-conditioned units — circles the whole island of Oahu several times a day, it provides a pleasant four-hour ride along the continually changing shoreline of the glistening emerald-green Pacific. The rays of Hawaii's seemingly special kind of sunshine will shoot new life into your aging bones, and do more for you than if you were to corner the Geritol market and drink it dry.

Like most people, I read advice columns. One on retirement expostulated the merits of keeping peace in the family should you and your partner be the only ones left in the nest. It suggested you get two TV sets and place each one in a different room, so that you could each have your own daily program.

Spend the heavenly summer days and evenings in the womb of a TV room? Horrors! When I'm finally free of my structured life, I'm going to drink copiously of everything I've looked at so enviously for years; unrestricted holidays and the ultimate pleasure of changing, upon a whim, night into day or day into night.

I'll play it *my* way, right up to the Pearly Gates. There'll be no rocking chairs, shawls or TV guides to clutter up my new pathway. It'll be on with the Dance of Life for me.

THE LANGUAGE OF AGING

by Fred Kerner

"Retirement," said Ernest Hemingway, "is the most loathsome word in the English language." Papa Hemingway never made it to age sixty-five, so he never found out that there are much more odius insults directed at Seniors among the more than half-million words in our vocabulary.

Once we reach the state of being old, our language betrays us through its colloquialisms. For example, we are told to "Act your age!" or, "You're over the hill." And I've been gently reminded that I'm on "the downward slide."

Suddenly I find that I'm being ushered into and out of places ahead of the attractive woman I'm with. "Age," they tell me, "before beauty." The list goes on — discouragingly.

The very word "old" denotes a negativistic attitude. We get a picture of something that is falling apart. Something to be thrown away. Something useless and decrepit. In a word, old.

Yet the *Dictionary of Canadian English* — which, interestingly enough, bears the sub-title "The Senior Dictionary" only once defines old as being worn out, among the many definitions it lists for the adjective. Other definitions include:

- Having existed long; aged: *an old wall.*
- Of age; in age: *the baby is one year old.*
- Not new; made long ago; ancient: *an old excuse, an old tomb.*
- Much worn by age or use: *old clothes.*
- Looking or seeming old; mature: *old for her years.*
- Having much experience: *being old in wrongdoing.*
- Former: *an old student came back to visit his teacher.*
- Earlier or earliest: *Old English.*
- Familiar; dear: *good old fellow.*

Note that the definition likening one to "old clothes" comes about halfway down in order of preferred usage. One assumes that lexicographers recognize that just being old doesn't necessarily wear out the human machine or spirit. But, as Garson Kanin once pointed out, inactivity does.

In discussing the synonyms for old, even the *DCE* manages to stick the knife in. "Old," the editors add at this point, "means not young, but near the end of life," and it goes on to give as synonyms, "dilapidated, decayed, shabby, outworn."

Seeing all these terms in print, suggests perhaps that more damage is done by the written word than by the spoken word. I felt no pain in passing the round-number barriers. I didn't wince when I reached thirty. Nor did I flinch on my fortieth birthday — but seeing myself referred to in print as having reached *that* pinnacle threw me.

Many months later, after I had written a newspaper series for a major U.S. syndicate, my editor sent me the first tearsheets. And there on the front page of the *Chicago Tribune* was a boxed note, labelled, "About the Author." I started to read it with the pleasure of literary parenthood until I realized the first sentence began: "Fred Kerner, forty-year-old author and journalist . . ." My wife tells me I went into a brown state from which I didn't recover for several weeks.

E.T.
THE ELDERLY TERRESTRIAL

RESTRICTED

| 65 YRS |
| AND |
| OVER |

SHE IS ALONE
SHE IS AFRAID
SHE DOESN'T HAVE AN INDEXED PENSION

An elderly terrestrial is abandoned in a hostile society, where she is condemned to live in a closet and eat nothing but Reese's Pieces. She is rescued by a small group of children who realize that she is wiser and better than they are.

It was the power of the written word that all but destroyed me, not my advanced years. Then I remembered what Satchel Paige, the ever-youthful baseball pitcher, once said: "How old would you be if you didn't know how old you was?"

When my doctor examined me a short time ago, took X-rays, pinched and probed, but could find nothing wrong, though I complained of a painful heel, he said, "You'll just have to grin and bear it. These things happen when we get older."

"*We!*" I thought, looking at the forty-year-old whippersnapper's totally grey hair — mine is still barely tinged with a few white strands. "We!"

"What do you mean, 'These things happen'?" I rejoined, in my best what-kind-of-doctor-are-you tone. "My other heel is doing just fine and it's the same age as the one that hurts."

So, you see, "old" is too frequently used in a derogatory manner. Witness: "dirty old man" or "old goat." I was always under the impression that lasciviousness was a symptom of lechery, not of advanced years, otherwise I guess I was old when I was twenty!

"Little old ladies in tennis shoes." Why Adidas are a target for aspersions is beyond the scope of my understanding. But the phrase has come to refer to narrow-minded and persnickety persons — female or not — whose perspective is no bigger than a thimble.

"Old fogey." A fogey is one who is behind the times or lacks enterprise. I know a great many young people who fall into this category.

"Old maid." Similar to the lady in tennis shoes; a fussbudget, a finicky pest.

"Old woman." This expression is generally used to describe a gossip, a chatterbox — whether female or male.

And then there's that sneering "sugar daddy"; no need to use "old" in connection with this one. The dictionary — yes, the conservative Canadian one! — says a sugar daddy is "a wealthy old man who lavishes gifts and money on a younger woman in return for her favours." With *going dutch* a common way of life in this age of feminism, the sugar daddy must be a phenomenon that has had its day.

There are a whole string of conversational references that contain insidious prejudice against aging:

- She looks good for her age.
- He's too old to be doing that.
- Past his prime.
- In her dotage.

They go on and on. The next time someone tells me that I'm not getting any older, I'm just getting better . . . I'll crown him or her with a nugget of Golden Age.

I haven't disregarded the fine words, though. There are "ripening," "mellowing," "seasoning," "seniority," "flower of age," "age of responsibility," "maturity," "full age," "coming of age," and "reaching one's majority."

But basically, with language as the opponent, we spar daily with the negative suggestions that age is our worst enemy.

An American newspaper columnist once suggested that a word be coined to describe all of us who have passed the magical sixty — or midlife, as I prefer to think of it. He suggested we call these people genarians — a kind of shortcut for sexagenarians, septuagenarians, octogenarians or nonagenarians. And those specific terms of genarianship should, he said, be abbreviated to sexos, septos, octos, and nons. I'm delighted to be a sexo — gives me the sort of image I've always wanted to cultivate.

Pianist Arthur Rubinstein was probably closest to the truth when he said, "When I was young, I used to have successes with women because I was young. Now I have successes with women because I am old. Middle-age was the hard part."

READING
BETWEEN THE LINES

We are all forced to listen to double-talk at one time or another, and Seniors are no exception. Here is a brief guide to some of the most common metaphors you're likely to hear.

When they say:	They really mean:
What do you expect at your age?	Stop complaining and consider yourself lucky.
Wow, you're looking great for your age!	Wow, I didn't think you were still alive!
It's important to keep your sense of humour.	I've got bad news for you.
Are you getting tired yet?	You're beginning to get on my nerves.
The doctor will re-evaluate you in the morning.	The doctor has tickets for the ball game.
Let me know if there's anything I can do for you.	But don't make a habit of it.
Do you need to go to the bathroom?	Is it too late to go to the bathroom?
That's amazing!	That's impossible!
That's incredible!	That's impossible!
That's impossible!	I can't believe a word you say!

HOW TO AVOID "HOW TO" BOOKS

by George W. Powell

When a man gets to be my age — which I intend to do shortly — he understandably resents all those "My! You're looking younger than *ever!*" gushings tinged with mock surprise; it's a clear indication the gushee has reached the prime of senility in the gusher's mind. But there's an even greater late-in-life irritation to which most of us are sooner or later exposed: all those "How To" books for the care and preservation of Golden Agers.

Maybe it's because I'm such a slow reader. In any event, I'd hardly finished ploughing through a voluminous *How to Survive The Male Mid-Life Crisis* when family and friends started inundating me with reading material I thought would be more appropriate for the *next* crisis down the road. Retirement! Alas, tempus had indeed fugitted, and there I was knee-deep in such esoterica as *How to Budget for Golden Age Independance*, *How to Be a Hale and Hearty Senior Citizen*, *How to Discover Sex Begins at Sixty*, *How to Adjust Emotionally for the Golden Years*, *How to Hatch Your Nest Egg NOW!*, and a whole raft of more "How To's" than you'd know how to shake an OAS application form at.

Just what *is* the nature of the retirement beast? There are those who would have us believe that retirement means nothing more than drinking coffee on our own time, or a stage of life when we're no longer too busy to talk about how busy we are. Some say it is the time when we never do all the things we intended to do when we'd have the time, as well as a logical time to remember that the time you *enjoy* wasting is not wasted time. In short, it's a timely time to procrastinate, because without procrastination a lot of us wouldn't have anything much to do. "When a man retires and time is no longer a matter of urgent importance, nine times out of ten he'll be presented with a timepiece." — *TIME* Magazine.

There may be more poetry than justice in poetic justice, but there's enough of both in the fact that the future still comes only one day at a time, and that with a modicum of talent and an abundance of chutzpah, a Golden Ager need not experience the onset of phobophobia (the fear of being afraid) in making his/her lifestyle decision, and certainly need not be afraid of phobophobophobia (the fear of the fear of being afraid) setting in. As a precaution at this stage, however, one should be quite convinced that the light seen at the end of the tunnel isn't attached to an oncoming train.

Invitation to the Dance

Obviously, any belated lifestyle decisions reflect a lack of preparation for retirement. Too many of us, it would seem, wanted to save ourselves for the Senior Prom, but forgot that somewhere along the way we'd have to learn how to dance. Hence, Rule Number One: Master at least a few basic steps if you hope to waltz through the Golden Years.

The Fitness Fox Trot

"Health Means Wealth" is the bromide those "How To-ers" sprinkle so liberally among their scribblings in urging Seniors to exercise, how to eat "a sensible diet," and indeed, become involved in anything else that might keep the body ticking over with or without the aid of stewed prunes. One popular and most apposite retort in this connection, which you'll never see quoted in their sententious scenarios, is "When you're pushing seventy, that's all the exercise you need!" Speaking as one who has not indulged in any form of calisthenics since discharge (honourable) from the military in 1945, the tedious "to exercise, or not to exercise" quandary is best resolved as follows:

- In the case where one hears "Snap, Crackle & Pop" first thing every morning, and it *isn't* one's cereal, then one might consider a mild form of exercise until the noise abates.
- In all other cases, Golden Agers should adopt the commendable practice of Jerome K. Jerome: "Whenever I feel the urge to exercise, I lie down until the feeling wears off."

The credibility of "good diet equals good health" was laid to rest years ago when it was widely reported a sprightly centenarian had been asked to what he attributed his longevity, and that worthy had forthrightly replied: "I don't know yet. I'm still dickering with three breakfast food companies to see who'll pay the most for an endorsement."

Nevertheless, at a time of life when we no longer feel the need to sacrifice our appetite on the altar of appearance, the do-gooders take the line that we should starve ourselves to death in order to live longer. Such outdated thinking harks back to the days when an apple a day kept the doctor away — not the threat of a malpractice suit.

"Eat natural foods!" they urge, fully aware that at our age we need all the preservatives we can get. "Watch your waistline!" they exhort us, as though putting on too much weight might result in your being arrested for unlawful assembly. What they do *not* explain is that when a 220-pound man (if you'll excuse a personal reference) laughs, twice as much of him is having a good time as when a 110-pound man laughs. Why, I ask you, in these our reclining years, should we pleasantly plump people abandon our *embonpoints* and deny ourselves opportunity to fully rise to life's few remaining risible occasions? Those who foster the fitness fad suggest that it's better to be over the hill than under it. After all, we were once worried about being middle aged — but we outgrew that, too.

The Recreation Rhumba

"Keep active! Think young!" That's the double-barreled and questionable formula our self-appointed counsellors would foist on us to stimulate our allegedly torpid minds. They recommend what they cleverly label

"Participaction," meaning active participation for us in *inter alia* educational courses, travel, and such esoteric pastimes as tatting, whist, croquet and gardening. This flies in the face of William Allen White's celebrated advice to the Women's Club of America: "Raise more hell and fewer dahlias."

The theory behind all this, it should be carefully noted, is that we're too relaxed, and therefore the therapy required is to keep busy. On the other hand, should we keep ourselves busy, our mentors then insist the therapy is to relax. In short, our retirement playground is to provide a see-saw sort of existence as we put ourselves through hoops to swing from relaxing busily to being busily relaxed.

Make no mistake about it; leisure can indeed prove a challenging responsibility. But insofar as more education is concerned, most of us — already over-educated in so many things that we don't need to know — are quite content to live off our intellectual fat.

And then there's travel. That inexpensive travel does indeed provide an opportunity for Seniors to acquire an air of confidence and a patina of sophistication was recently reaffirmed by an elderly resident of Four Corners, Saskatchewan, who stoutly announced: "The missus an' me went around the world for our holiday this year, but next year we're gonna go someplace else."

The definitive response to Participaction pushers is to be found in a statement by the formidable Lady Astor, made at the age of eighty: "I used to dread to think of getting old," she confessed, "because I thought I would not be able to do all the things I wanted. But now that I'm older I find I don't want to do them." The defence rests.

The Sex Samba

"The Myth and Reality of Sex in the Later Years" is almost a standard article for the longest chapter in those "How To" books. Its pages not only assure us there is no physiological reason for Golden Agers to abandon sex, but also rather strongly hint we should be making love as though we were an endangered species — this without taking into account that sex might have abandoned *us*. Surely a more realistic view was voiced by a former prime

Cartoon by Graham Harrop

minister of Canada when he averred: "There is no place for Golden Agers in the bedrooms of the nation — *sauf pour faire dodo.*"

Using my own libido as a criterion, I'd say these writers are inclined to confuse their fantasized "reality" with their (alas) factual "myth"; that is, they see our vice *versa*, as it were. While they emphasize sex is a game that need never be called off because of darkness, they fail to mention it is often called off because so many of our vintage are concerned about being prematurely "called off" to play in the Elysian Fields. We simply must view any such divertissement as a potential sudden-death game — a pointless goal, even if we *are* condemned to live only with memories of past scores. This is but one of the many frustrations of having young blood in an old container, heightened, as it is, by the fact that abstinence makes the heart grow fonder.

It was in much the same context that a Golden Oldie husband finally succumbed (in the *non*-fatal sense) to his wife's wish for a second honeymoon, during which she hoped they'd harbour the ardour and capture the rapture experienced the first time around. Hubby had expressed serious doubts about any such outcome for this ambitious project, all of which she summarily dismissed with: "Why not, if your constitution is up to it?" "My constitution is fine," Hubby was to reply with a sigh. "It's my preamble I'm worried about!"

Regrettably, while you'll find many a peppy preface in those "How To" books, there seldom is heard an encouraging word for languishing preambles, such as reviving animal magnetism to libidinous levels with Yohimbine Hydrochloride — a Stanford University scientist's promising amatory aid — the first *real* aphrodisiac, still in the experimental stage but already producing mounting interest in rodent circles. Under these circumstances how can one reasonably hope for respect in the morning?

Mind you, there *are* one or two of these authors who look on us all as if we'd played leap-frog with a unicorn during pubescent years; that we'd lived through the Sexual Revolution without even getting wounded, and are unlikely to suffer so much as a sexy scratch from here to eternity. On the other hand, the vast majority of them seem to believe we can perform six impossible things before breakfast (in fact, a Dr. Havelook Ellis plans to market a pair of Golden Ager dolls — Barbara and Kenneth Venerable.

"They won't need batteries," the good doctor enthuses. "They're *always* turned on!") and point out that at sixty-nine or thereabouts a Senior is not only capable of being named in a paternity suit, but it *could* be a class action. Young and virile lads involved in such litigation are usually said to have "machismo," this automatically translates into "dirty old man" for their Golden Age counterparts.

This brand of "How To-er" serves to raise our hope (if little else) by suggesting that reTIREment can be reFIREment if you're still reasonably mobile and your engine doesn't rattle when engaged in low gear — which is like saying that one can be rich if one is up-to-here in money. Quite frankly, I'd give ten-to-one odds that, save for a few lukewarm embers still among us, most of our fires went out about the same time our backs did, and that we must now go to Florida to be in heat.

We have only to be reminded that our once erotic invitation to "blow in my ear" lost much of its raunchy appeal when we were obliged to add "if a hearing-aid doesn't turn you off." But then, so much has changed in the sexual arena for Golden Oldies since our gladiatorial days; nowadays, it would seem, the attitude is that it's easier to pray for forgiveness than to resist temptation, which suggests that parents of the Today Generation aren't of the same forbidding breed up with which *we* had to put. In our impermissive society, even the *word* "s-x" was a no-no.

This whole, broad subject is admittedly a complex one, but if the flood of sex information swirling about Golden Agers were to be distilled, it would boil down to but one sentence of irrefutable logic: "Use what Mother Nature has given you before Father Time takes it away." Tennis, anyone?

The Financial Fandango

In providing advice on money matters, our "How To" friends all too often fail to give the other side of the coin, so to speak. They preach a purse-strings sermon, for example, that cautions: "While it's true you can't take it with you, be certain you have enough left to get there." This in an inflationary era when "a dollar to a doughnut" is considered an even bet, the "$64,000 Question" TV show had to be replaced by "The Million Dollar Chance of a Lifetime," and a fool is defined as someone who holds on to his money!

While at pains to stress that money alone cannot buy retirement happiness, our would-be guides do not mention it *will* pay for a top-notch research team to resolve that problem for you. "Insist on living within your income!" they commendably counsel, but without ever adding "even if you have to borrow to do it" as a practical safeguard against bare feet or worse. Their sins of omission transcend transgression.

These "How To-ers" attempt to thrust home their message in a number of ways. One will emphasize that it takes a lot more money to be poor nowadays than it did a mere decade ago. Another cites the "sad but true story" of Mr. John Doe on his eve of retirement. Mrs. Doe, he relates, suggested it might be wise to set up a budget, to which Mr. Doe replied: "OK, dear. Let's start with the basics; there's food, shelter and clothing. We have a choice of two." The implication is clear. Life in a retirement teepee isn't going to be a heap of fun without at least a little wampum — although this will come as news to a limited number of aging braves and squaws.

Nor is their advice on investment much more electrifying. Here we have yet another "sad but true" account of an impulsive retiree who sank all his savings into the acquisition of a mink farm. "And all the mink turned out to be gay!" the author triumphantly concludes this tale of woe, presumably intent on crushing any entrepreneurial spirit we might harbour. Decades ago, Billy Rose delivered much the same message, albeit more succinctly: "Never invest in anything that eats or needs repainting" — both principles of which he violated in one fell swoop by marrying again.

How, then, to best use our current cash crop as seed money for future financial harvests? Why, plough it into annuities and RRSP funds, our advisors advise, seemingly ignorant of the fact that the paid-up annuity we bought back in 1950 now provides the princely sum of $48.72 every passing month, or that when our RRSP ship comes in, the revenue department will be there to dock it.

In truth, the best advice for preserving one's financial resources hasn't materially changed since the Phoenicians invented money; work hard, work long, and use double-entry bookkeeping (i.e., two sets of books).

There is a cookie-cutter picture of Seniors to be found in advertising these days; white-haired, glowing-with-health individuals, smiling as they stand square-shouldered in front of their modest yet trim Bide-A-Wee retreats. The accompanying copy might be hawking anything from relief for varicose veins to services of Pre-Arrangement Centres — the latest euphemism for a business undertaking that thrives and survives because people don't. Whatever the message, the implication is that all retirees have common hopes, fears, wants, needs, dreams, bank balances and loose-denture problems.

It is true that as a group of individuals some of us might share the same sentiments — the feeling we have reached a certain age long before our time. For example, we have the thought that the future isn't what it used to be, and even the wistful hope that the handwriting on the wall could be a forgery.

But it's also true that the only time *all* Golden Agers share the *same* sentiment is when they're uprooted from "normal" life to inhabit the strange new world of retirement. That's when each and every one of us is mysteriously endowed with a philosophical attitude that — by happenstance or breeding — reflects the exemplary outlook of one of our forebears when being uprooted from the Garden of Eden.

"All ribbing aside, Eve," he reportedly said, "After all, we *do* live in an age of transition. Eh?"

SEX AFTER SIXTY
by Rae Thomas

In our house, the phrase "making the earth move" now means that a front loader is working in the back yard. The earth-shaking Richter scale heights of passion have been replaced by mere trembles and low scale readings. Gone are the days when the sex act, or even the thought of it, interrupted breakfast, lunch, dinner or dish washing.

Now, only the latest headlines or a favourite TV show dare intrude upon our retirement solitude. Formerly, a raised eyebrow or a knowing nod catapulted me to the bathroom in search of my favourite cologne. Today, the raised eyebrow could mean anything from slipping eyeglasses to a low stock market quotation or a signal that the late movie is over.

Where has my robust rooster of earlier years gone? What happened to that soft bed of leaves in the countryside and the down filled sleeping bag we used on camping trips? Now our only contact with leaves is with rake and wheelbarrow!

A long walk with another over-sixty girlfriend gives me an opportunity to exchange recipes and stories about grandchildren. Eventually, when we've run out of recipes and stories, our conversation turns to sex.

"Henry is canned," my friend Mary says.

"Canned — you mean in jail?"

"No, he's impotent. Just when I'm free of the worry of getting pregnant, I find out I can't even enjoy a good roll in the hay."

But when *I* get home — hey, wouldn't you know! — there's the familiar raised eyebrow and nod of the head. Am I seeing things? No. He's wide awake. I dive for the bathroom and my cologne; into the bedroom to put on my slinky peach satin gown, exuding magnolia blossom. Will the earth move tonight?

Jeanette MacDonald and Maurice Chevalier share an amorous moment.

FAMOUS SENIORS

by Nicholas Pashley

Jane Ellen Harrison once said, "Old age, believe me, is a good and pleasant time." Yet we all dread it. Well, it's not surprising, when you look at expressions like "old age," "elderly," and the like. At least words like "codger" and "geezer" have a sort of raffish quality to them. The medical profession has invented a good euphemism for old age: later maturity. Now *that's* more like it. There's dignity in later maturity.

In any case, it's all relative, isn't it? As Bernard Baruch said, "I will never be an old man. To me, old age is always fifteen years older than I am." And he was eighty-five when he said it!

Age in this century has always had a bad rap. "Only the good die young," we are told. What nonsense. Adherents of the youth-is-beautiful school persist in telling us about Mozart, Schubert, Keats, Marilyn Monroe, and James Dean, all of whom died before their fortieth birthday. General Custer never saw forty either, but there were extenuating circumstances in his case. Plenty of very competent people have lived to ripe old ages: Pythagoras, Sophocles, Michaelangelo, Matisse, Verdi, Monet, Benjamin Franklin, Thomas Jefferson, Voltaire, Susan B. Anthony, Freud, and Jung all lived well into their eighties. Mahatma Gandhi was shot at seventy-eight,

Sir Winston
and Lady Spencer Churchill

an age Galileo came damn close to, despite his troubles with the Inquisition. Haydn hit seventy-seven and might have gone longer had Napoleon not invaded Vienna in what proved to be the last month of the composer's life. Samuel Pepys managed seventy years, surviving both the Great Plague and the Great Fire of London.

Money often equals longevity. It should not be surprising that a good many rich folk hit the high numbers: John Jacob Astor, Andrew Carnegie, Henry Ford, and William Randolph Hearst made it into their eighties. Conrad Hilton and John D. Rockefeller, among others, lived past ninety, demonstrating the value of hard cash in living a long life.

Clearly, hungry people die earlier. But the affluent twentieth century has been a hotbed of longevity. Eminent souls like Winston Churchill, Albert Schweitzer, Frank Lloyd Wright, G.B. Shaw, Pablo Picasso, Bertrand Russell, and Marc Chagall cruised past ninety, and Eubie Blake and Grandma Moses made a mockery of the biblical four score and ten by sailing past one hundred.

Okay, so you've started collecting your pension and you're feeling all washed up. Forget it! George Burns was born in 1896, is probably old enough to be your father, and he's still earning a living. Don Ameche and Milton Berle are almost as old as the twentieth century, and Irving Berlin was already a brash kid in the streets of New York when the rest of *them* were born. In fact, he wrote "Alexander's Ragtime Band" over seventy-five years ago!

George Burns

The current pensioner is in good company. Helen Hayes, Bob Hope, Sir John Gielgud, Barbara Stanwyck, Katherine Hepburn, Lucille Ball, Burt Lancaster, Joe Dimaggio, Frank Sinatra, Walter Cronkite, and Liberace, to name but a few, could be collecting their monthly cheques. Sam Snead, Byron Nelson, and Ben Hoagan were all born in 1912, and they're still playing better golf than most other people. Throw in Gene Sarazen and you've got an impressive foursome. And if you're just now crossing that great Social Security divide, you will be joined by other new pensioners like Cyd Charisse, Louis Jourdan, Deborah Kerr, Maureen O'Hara, Jane Russell, Betty Friedan, Allan Ginsberg, John

Katherine Hepburn

Cary Grant

Glenn, Yves Montand, Peter Ustinov, and Skeezix from Gasoline Alley. These people will soon be followed by Charles Bronson, Jackie Cooper, Ava Gardner, Kurt Vonnegut, Rodney Dangerfield, George McGovern, and Helen Gurley Brown (don't tell her you heard it from me). And it looks like Chuck Berry will be the first rock'n'roller in the Social Security Hall of Fame.

All right then. You've entered what we've decided to call "later maturity." You've been caught in the crossfire of "mandatory retirement." What now? Are you just going to fade away? Not in the 1980s you're not. Remember, idle hands are the devil's playground. If the conventional workplace no longer has a place for you, set your sights a little higher. As we have seen, the world of showbiz does not discriminate against the older practitioner — but it may require previous experience. When George Burns turned sixty-five he already had fifty-eight years of working experience. If you've spent the last forty-five years in an office, you might find the transition to the bright lights a little jarring. Your buck and wing, to be quite frank, might not be what it once was, and maybe you don't look so hot in tights these days.

Not to worry. How about something you can do sitting down? In 1984, Helen Hoover Santameyer went to the top of the bestseller lists at the age of eighty-eight. Playwright Ben Travers had three plays running in London when he turned ninety. P. G. Wodehouse published his last book at ninety-three. Goethe finished *Faust* at eighty-one. Writing is an ideal pastime for the later mature and, in fact, many of our most successful living writers are Seniors. Harold Robbins, Saul Bellow, William Burroughs, Eudora Welty, Simone de Beauvoir, James Michener, Samuel Beckett, Isaac Bashevis Singer, Morley Callaghan, Irving Stone, and Jorge Luis Borges are all at least seventy. And look at Graham Greene. He made quite a name for himself over the years while writing five hundred words a day, every day. In later years this figure has dropped to three hundred. That's not many words. Imagine yourself Graham Greene, sitting in Antibes, knocking off a measly three hundred words a day. Can't be bad, can it?

Other creative folk work longer than the rest of us are allowed to. Look at film directors. D. W. Griffith worked until he died at seventy-three, and Alfred Hitchcock at eighty-one. John Huston, David Lean, Ingmar Bergman, and Federico Fellini, are all still directing *and* cashing their cheques.

Artists and musicians also continue long beyond the age of mandatory retirement. Henry Moore and Salvador Dali can sell their work any day of the week. And do you think Jascha Heifetz, Claudio Arrau, Vladimir Horowitz, or Ella Fitzgerald would be able to fill Carnegie Hall tomorrow? You bet your denture cream they could!

Maybe you're not the artistic sort. *Nihil desperandum*, as they say. Perhaps the field of religion is more up your alley. The wisdom of maturity has long been respected in theological circles. While the founder of Christianity died young, Confucius hit seventy-two and Gautama Buddha seventy-nine — not bad for the fifth century BC. In more recent times, Mary Baker Eddy lived to eighty-nine, Joseph Smith, the founder of the Church of Latter Day Saints, was shot at thirty-eight, but subsequent Mormons have preferred older men. Ezra Taft Benson, the current president, prophet, seer, and revelator is eighty-six. Jehovah's Witnesses don't celebrate birthdays, so don't send a card to President Frederick W. Franz who reaches ninety-three this year. The Ayatollah Khomeini was born in 1901 but he didn't become what he is today until he was seventy-eight. The present Pope is remarkably youthful as Popes go, having attained a full pensionable age only in 1985. The estimable Mother Theresa is another decade older, where Billy Graham and Oral Roberts both saw the light (of day) in 1918.

But what if your company doesn't want you any more? Fine. So take over the government and raise their taxes. To this day, politics still provides a number of opportunities for those who are considered too mature to perform other jobs. The safest such jobs tend to go to members of royal families. Take Emperor Hirohito of Japan, a sprightly eighty-five, or Norway's King Olav V, born in 1903. You don't have to be from one of the major families. Who's ever heard of Tonga's King Taufa'ahau Tupou IV or King Melietoa Tanumafili of Western Samoa? The drawback, of course, is that if you're not royal now, you're not likely to become royal unless you can prove that you were stolen from your cradle and that you are none other than Prince Franz Joseph II of Liechtenstein or Grand Duke Jean of Luxembourg.

On the other hand, you could marry into royalty. The Queen Mother, who was born in 1900, did just that and she still looks great. Prince Philip, a brand new pensioner in 1986, has done quite nicely for himself as well. Mind you, it may be difficult to make a good royal marriage at your age.

Still, you don't have to be regal to be important. Take Ronald Reagan. Remember when Jack Kennedy got elected all those years ago, and suddenly politics seemed a young man's game? Well, Reagan is now more than five years older than any American president has ever been. Reagan, of course, has triggered all sorts of *ageist* jokes and unfair references to senility. However, being unable to distinguish between Vienna and Vietnam or Bolivia and Brazil, doesn't make him senile. He's just dumb, and you can be dumb at any age. Ronald Reagan was in his fifties before he had even the roughest idea of where Vietnam was. One could find plenty of eight-year-olds who would have trouble with Bolivia and Brazil, but not many eight-year-olds would call the Princess of Wales "Princess David." Not in public, anyway.

The interesting thing about mature world leaders is that they tend to be a bit extreme, leaning very strongly to either one side or the other. Let's look at the Lefties. China's Deng Xiaoping, East Germany's Erich Honecker, Hungary's Janos Kadar, North Korea's Kim Il-Sung, and Romania's Nicolae Ceausescu are all well over sixty-five, and represent the traditional approach of the socialist world. The conspicuous exception is the stunningly youthful Mikhail Gorbachev, a lad in his mid-fifties who probably has to ask President Gromyko or Premier Tikhonov for the car on a Saturday night.

Meanwhile, on the right wing, step forward Presidents Alfredo Stroessner of Paraguay and Augusto Pinochet of Chile, both of whom are over seventy.

So now *you're* a Senior. Why not cash your pension cheque and plan a little party. You can invite some fellow pensioners to join you — party types like Cary Grant, Fred Astaire and Ginger Rogers, Gene Kelly, and Lena Horne, if you can get them. But they might not want to hang out with kids like you.

And, while you're partying, remember the words of jazz great Eubie Blake on his hundredth birthday. "These docs, they always ask you how you live so long. I tell 'em, 'If I'd known I was gonna live this long, I'd have taken better care of myself.' "

I'll be Frank, you be Earnest

The President
Space Services Inc.
Houston, Texas

Sir:

    At first I thought you had gone off your rocket. But, no. Your idea of an orbiting cemetary is fabulous, and I'd sure like to be the first one to be sent into space, circling the earth for sixty-eight million years in a shiny crypt that will be seen by relatives and friends through powerful telescopes. But the trouble is, I'm only 70, and I can't see myself being dead in time for the first launch. The doc tells me I've got the best circulation for a man my age he's ever seen.

    In any case, some day my chance will come, and when cremated to a fare-thee-well, I'll be joining the countless ash people already in orbit.

    I fervently hope, too, that once fitted with a new body, the Lord, on Resurrection Day, will allow me to go on my merry way for the better part of eternity. There's so much of Earth I haven't seen. Besides, the idea of meeting a zillion plus people and hearing a continuum of harp music isn't my cup of tea.

    I note that the price of cremation and a gold-coloured capsule is $3,900. Seeing it's not everybody's luck to be as rich as the Hunt brothers, would it be possible for you to put out a no-frills capsule and advertise it as the Ashcan Junket?

    Meanwhile, I wish you every success and hope you don't meet with too much stiff competition.

Sincerely,

Frank B. Ricard

ON BECOMING A CHARACTER

by Elizabeth Ruggier

To wake up one morning and discover that, overnight, somehow you've turned seventy is sobering. But it's alright so long as there are a few people around to breathe incredulously and flatteringly, " I *don't* believe it!"

It's those others who, no less well-intentioned, insist that the years don't matter because you're so wonderfully full of character, especially about the face! *That* makes you feel like a bag lady complete with bulging paper carrier bags crammed with memories, insights, the tattered remnants of a thousand false starts, and stuffed down there somewhere, a slender dog-eared and almost illegible dossier inscribed "Accomplishments." It's discouraging. But not for long, because about the same time it dawns on you that you have a choice. You can either abandon yourself to the excesses of the "before and after septuagenarianism" identity crisis or you can go with the flow. That is, you can accept the role apparently being cast for you on the strength of a lined face and a lively, at times even ascerbic, wit and become a character. Not a bad option given that it presents the opportunity to shed the anonymity of the early and middle years of life and go for a ranking character status with its promise of a ready audience for all your henceforth privileged doings and sayings. Surely nobody with half an ego could resist that.

My job (retirement is not for me) calls for a certain amount of travelling each year. Lately, my schedule was heavier than usual. It started with a trip to Hong Kong for a trade fair with a stop-over in Tokyo to pick up some Japanese translations and — sandwiched in between — nightly visits to Shanghai and Peking.

My eagerness to go ahead with the trip was taken as evidence of an indomitable spirit, rather as though, quixotically, I was undertaking the arduous task of crossing the Pacific by covered wagon.

A grey-haired and mature aspect tends to illicit immediate repect in the Orient, where they still cling to the anti-diluvian notion that if you've been around long enough, you've earned it! From Tokyo's Ginza to Hong Kong — where the neon outshines Las Vegas — to the shabby splendour of Peking's Forbidden City, the respect was overwhelming. While it might have been balm to a bruised spirit, it quickly proved rather more irritating to an independent — not to mention indomitable — one! There was no way I could give the credible "character" performance, being relegated, as it were, to the slow lane Oriental style.

A month later I was in Milan on a regular business trip. What a pleasure. The Italians are not only robust people, they are also *all* characters. So I was among equals, competitively but enjoyably.

Frankfurt was the next stop. In Germany, characters, it seems, are like hen's teeth, non-existent. Therefore, there is no recognition. It's amazing how quickly one can learn to expect recognition and how dismaying it is to be without it.

You're wondering how I could expect to score in countries where I might have language difficulties and where cultural differences make for distinctive determinants. Well, let me tell you, characters are like children. They recognize each other and regardless of language *can* communicate. Not perhaps in so many words — it's hard to explain but it does happen.

I was born in England, the home of eccentricity, and have debated the difference between eccentricity and character. There is a difference. Despite the claims of some to the contrary, in England where the class system still flourishes, true eccentricity is a class affair. Beloved of the aristocracy,

Famous Eccentric, Jean Rhys

from the peerage on down, it has even been known to exist among the ultra-suburbanite Royals.

It is lastly a matter of dress and comportment. Some see it as an expression of dissention, which is nonsense. The English, as a whole, consider themselves so ineffably right that they are largely unaware of differing points of view. They must be the only people in the world who, finding themselves in a country other than their own, regard its nationals as foreigners.

Characters, by contrast, especially in North America, come from all walks of life. They're bubble-bursters and, in their own way, social commentators. They don't give a damn and say so. And provided they do it entertainingly enough, they are applauded for it. On the whole they are indistinguishable from the community at large so far as dress and comportment are concerned. But they do enjoy a special recognition.

By now I was feeling very much at home with my role which, it was becoming increasingly clear, was permitting me the luxury of staying in the fast lane with the major advantages of the slow lane. For one, I was still in the swim, I didn't have to fight to make it upstream. With little, if anything, to prove, I was turning out to be something of a public relations asset. Nobody had to fear losing their job to me. Mine existed because I *had it*. That's why the Scandinavian tour I did later in the year was set up especially for me.

That I opted to do it by train, travelling on a Eurail Pass, was a little unexpected and was regarded by a few as insanity. The majority, however, saw it as yet further proof of my youthful spirit. As it turned out, it was neither particularly adventurous nor taxing. But then how taxing can First Class be? In fact it was relaxing. Central stations tend to be in the centre of cities rather than twenty miles or so on their outskirts, as is the case with airports — a lot handier to hotels and other urban conveniences a traveller like me is usually seeking. The disadvantage is in the matter of luggage which, ideally should be as limited as possible since you mostly have to lug it yourself. The red cap, or porter as he is more familiarly known as in Europe, is as endangered a species there as he is here and indeed is already extinct in most places.

It was in Scandinavia that I got my comeuppance. They're all so healthy. Such a thing as a slow lane doesn't seem to exist.

I will not soon forget Stockholm. As I was preparing to clamber down from the train — a parachute would have been handy — my luggage was swept up by a lady, clearly my contemporary, who deposited it with one hand on the platform while she helped me down with the other. Mortifying!

In Oslo and Helsinki it was the same. I don't pretend to be in the best physical shape but heavens I'm not exactly doddering. Yet I came away from both of them wondering about myself. Only in Copenhagen did I get even close to recovering a degree of confidence. And I'm not sure why. Everybody there was just as formidably healthy. But they didn't seem to notice me in quite the same way. You might even say that I was overlooked.

I was glad there was nobody from home with me to witness the ignomony of my "defeat." I even toyed for a while with the idea of embarking on a physical rehabilitation program, but thankfully lost interest in it long before I could have done anything about it.

Back home, I told no one what had really happened, being content to bask in the admiration that came my way at yet another trip successfully concluded. I savoured their enjoyment of the tales with which I regaled them, especially when they left chuckling "what a character." Maybe after all role-playing is more appreciated here than anywhere else.

When I wake up one morning to find that overnight I've somehow turned eighty, it will be time, I think, to trade in my character status in favour of becoming a legend. A legend ensconced in a comfortable rural retreat but one that is not too far from the mainstream.

RETIRING FROM OFFICE
CONFESSIONS OF A CIVIL SERVANT
by G. Arthur Sage

My search for superannuation began in my late teens when I joined the public service, and my whole career was oriented towards an indexed pension to be garnished with the consulting contracts that arrive after retirement. All my contacts were in place, and I had quietly taken the backup discs from my office computer with the addresses of contacts and associates. So, when I went, I went quietly.

Of course, I was too ethical a man to go headlong into competition with my former employer. In fact, the conflict-of-interest guidelines demanded that I not deal with my former government and private sector contacts for a full year after retirement. So I'd take the long planned world cruise with my wife of forty years before sinking my teeth in earnest into the double-dipping system that so many of my former colleagues now inhabited.

I was now sixty-two years old and I had retired right on the nail of the "thirty plus fifty minus twenty-five formula" (thirty years of service — from twenty-two years of age to sixty-two — plus fifty-two years on the planet indexed to ten to make sixty). It was the kind of mathematics that separated a completely civil servant from the *polloi*. Only my income tax declaration was more incomprehensible. But, be that as it may, I was able to retire three years before I was sixty-five, and I wasn't arguing. After all, military pensions had admirals in retirement in their mid-thirties.

But recently, I'd heard rumours that the day would come when public servants would not have to retire at all! Who could possibly be that stupid when the world beckoned and, even with the urinary problems caused by the asbestos dust in the faulty office air-conditioning systems, you could still cruise the world with catheters and bags. What bliss to be really free without the stress and strain of the rat race.

But, after my retirement party and prior to our planned departure on the cruise, I had a few surprises. Mrs. Sage had been doing her own thing for forty years, and she was not used to having a strange man around the house after 7:30 in the morning. Moreover she resented it when I walked around the block with the dog to spy on the neighbours. The clock radio had always awakened us with soothing FM music interspersed with news bulletins and arts news, reassuring her that there was another hour for her to sleep in before the old man left the house.

Little things became difficult. A snoring lump lay beside her for an hour longer every morning. It wanted the main bathroom at the same time she did, and it didn't bring her coffee at 7:00. It shuffled around the kitchen making a mess and cursing when things weren't where they were meant to be. The FM station was switched to stock market reports on AM, interspersed with commercials that she loathed. And the murmur of its voice could be heard net-working with old cronies. The retirement of her husband, whom she loved dearly at a distance, would change her forever.

As for me, I had to get used to all kinds of little changes too. I had not bought cellotape for four decades and was shocked to find that it cost $1.99 per roll. Pens were no longer plentiful, and the cost of the morning newspaper was so much higher than it had been in 1946 when I'd last bought one. For a while, I regretted not being able to walk into my deputy ministerial office and find the papers of the day neatly arranged near the signature file. Accommodating these discoveries, as well as a renewed marriage relationship, took some time.

But, as things settled down, I realized that every day of the week was a Saturday. I rose in my own time and did not have to drive to work; nor did I have to open an urgent file full of problems; nor be summoned to urgent meetings or the minister's office to hear of yet another change in policy that I had to activate. I slowly started to speak English again, as words like "proactive," "interface," "maximatize," and "attributability" became incomprehensible to my new contacts. In place of reading *The Interim Procedural Guide to Evaluation Management Systems and their Effect on Human and Non-Human Resource Ecoconcerns*, I read *Wobegon Days* and *Fifth Business*. I even bought a copy of *Playboy* and discovered, while Mrs. Sage was at a fashion show for the local underprivileged, that there was fire in the old boy yet.

Often I contemplated all the years spent climbing the slippery pole to civil service success, always subordinate to someone, and always living in the knowledge that I was just a cog in the wheel. But the size of the wheel mattered, and I had become a senior cog in my mature years. I would never be famous, but that made no difference. I had no regrets as I glanced at the bronze plaque on my study wall celebrating twenty-five years of public service.

The house we had lived in for thirty years had served us well, but after the children were gone it was larger than necessary. Mrs. Sage felt, therefore, that a change of residence was due. She checked out houses for sale across the city, before setting her mind on a new condominium in a nice area known as "Tax Shelter Mews." It had two bedrooms with ensuite bathrooms, a rooftop lounge, patio, sundeck, marble and oak lobby, mirrored ceilings, and a sculptured marble waterfall in the atrium. The complex was "temperature efficiency controlled" and boasted a "state-of-the-art burglar detection system" connected to the sprinklers, so that the halls could be made instantly slippery, thus incapacitating intruders. However, I wasn't interested. I hated the idea of living inside someone else's concept — particularly after a life time of it.

I decided that I wanted to spend the rest of my days in the family home with its memories, smells, and secrets. I could fill any voids with books and pipe smoke, and was quite willing to buy my wife a grand piano if that made her feel better. But I had no intention of getting rid of any stuff that was the record of my life.

With some reluctance she agreed with me, as long as I agreed to rearrange the furniture and appliances to give the old home a new look. I had no problem with this idea, since I remembered the days of reorganization of government departments, which were not aimed at improvement but at satisfying a basic psychological need for a change every so often.

I see my retirement as a sabbatical. I will remain what I have always been — a public consultant. Only now, I can work at my own speed without the hindrances of the office, basking in the benefits of lucrative government contracts designed for "retired" deputy ministers.

I'll be Frank,
you be Earnest

Chic Electric Shaver Company
825 Close Shave Avenue
Toronto, Ontario

Dear Sir:

    Today is Father's Day -- a day on which good old
Dad realizes he's been clipped for $25 or so (no
reflection on your product) to pay for the gift his
brood has "touchingly" given him.

    Ordinarily, I must say that I am pleased with your
electric razor, because without it I would be a
patriarchal hippie. But recently I have been toying with
the idea of becoming one. Why? Because your razor is so
noisy that my wife, a sound sleeper with the disposition
of an enraged hornet when wakened ungently, has come
to think that I am running the lawnmower under her open
window when, in fact, I am in the bathroom shaving.

    Is there a chance that in the near future your
company will produce a truly noiseless electric razor?
As things stand now, my wife greets me daily by
planting a wooden kiss on my silken cheek, and then
tosses me an uncooked bone for breakfast. But then,
who could blame her?

    I look forward to your sharp response.

                        Yours very truly,

                            Frank B. Ricard

A NEW DEAL

BACKROOM SENIORS
MAKING POLITICS WORK FOR YOU
by Leonard L. Knott

There's more to retirement than afternoon bingo and cold ham and potato salad at Seniors' suppers. The obvious question is *what?* Millions of Golden Agers who were cast into oblivion at age sixty-five eagerly await the answer. Well, it's *politics*. No other form of recreation offers so much to mandatory retirees as this exciting, often shady and easy-to-learn pastime.

"Man is by nature a political animal," Aristotle said more than two thousand years ago. Confirmed male chauvinist that he was, he left out more than half the population who happened to be female. Twenty centuries later, their equally female descendants are proving to be just as politically animalistic as males. And that is a good thing for all of us Seniors, because in our social category women outnumber men almost two to one.

Gerontologists, whose job it is to study aging persons and help them live longer, aver that continued and even augmented mental activity is the secret of longevity. More important even than jogging! It's possible *that* scientific assertion might deter us from switching from country dancing to politicking. For most of us there was never any clear relationship between mental activity and political action. That's probably because our knowledge of the political world was limited to newspaper reports and TV coverage of elected legislators in action, or contact with arrogant and/or ignorant bureaucrats.

Governments at all levels, politicians in general, and the bureaucrats who work for them — tax collectors, postmen, customs inspectors and traffic cops — are the institutions and individuals we love to hate. Rarely do we hear of or see the backroom operations where our real enemies are.

The men and women we chose to represent us in the corridors of power were the ones that were exposed to public view. No sooner had they taken their oaths of office and shuffled off to their legislative seats than we were made aware that within our entire population no one equalled them for imbecility, general ineptitude and the innate ability to feather their own nests and those of their most intimate relatives.

This awareness was reinforced by the media who offered us such juicy tidbits as the report of the Canadian parliamentarian who complained about a senior appointment being bestowed upon one of his colleagues: "If they are looking for someone insignificant to stuff in the cabinet," he pleaded, "what about me?" What, indeed?

In our younger days, we discovered that legislators were men and women who couldn't manage their own affairs and made a fat living out of managing ours. What kept us from rising up and throwing them all out was the same excuse that kept us from writing books, composing master-pieces or acquiring degrees in jurisprudence: we were too busy earning a living and raising a family. We didn't have time.

Today, it's a brand new ball game. Seniors number in the millions. Our kids or their offspring are the ones without the time. We have Old Age Pensions, lower bus fares, and the greatest of all assets — twenty-four hours a day to do with exactly what we want.

Politics beckon. Will Rogers, who we all remember as a philosopher-comedian of the thirties, when philosophers were wise and comedians funny, once said: "All politics is apple sauce." Maybe so, but for a Senior for whom ham and potato salad has become a dietary staple, even apple sauce is enough to make the juices run. And keeping the juices running is what it's all about.

So let's give politics for Seniors a try. To those of us who are adventurous it offers many benefits. To mention only a few — a political attachment at the workshop level promises a way of:

- Terminating the careers of some of the more obnoxious politicians who have ridden on our backs for years and given us nothing but promises, promises . . .
- The establishment of an Old Boy/Old Girl network using the phone. (Nice to have phone calls other than those from magazine subscription agencies and funeral home solicitors.)
- Becoming somebody again (Mr. Mrs. Miss Ms.) instead of "that old timer up the street soon to be on his (her) way to the nursing home."
- Getting needed physical exercise as we demonstrate, congregate, dash from meeting to meeting and stuff fliers into letter boxes.
- Passing on our badly needed acquired knowledge and worldly experiences to audiences whose help will be useful in attaining our goals.
- Gaining, if not a livelihood, at least a few pittances in the form of free sandwiches and drinks, campaign pens, buttons, printed T-shirts and other political trinkets to add to our memorabilia.
- Protecting and enlarging our rights and privileges as Senior Citizens — including the right to more money. This cannot be left with any sense of security to any succeeding generation.
- Benefitting ourselves and all life's veterans by exposing and eventually eliminating threats to our trivial pursuits — such as driving a car after we're a hundred, gaining full employment at any age, and individual dignity and privacy.
- Providing a new source of jocular material with which to regale our fellow Seniors through our exposure to political chicanery and raucous backroom stories; glimpses of public persons' private peccadillos and endless free bus rides to remote locations where our presence makes up the numbers required to select or reject a candidate or policy.
- Paving the way to the ultimate goal — elective office where we may perpetuate our own brand of nonsense.

In short, nothing could be more rewarding for a time-surfeited retiree than a career in politics at any level. And that brings up an important point: where should an ambitious Senior, driven by lust for public service, set his

WE'D HAUE HAD MORE PEOPLE AT THE DEMONSTRATION
BUT MOST OF THEM WENT JOGGING ...

Cartoon by Graham Harrop

or her sights? It's not necessary, nor even practical, to aim for the top. Even though it is there that all the publicized perks are — decorator-designed offices, armored limousines with uniformed chauffeurs and police escorts, champagne dinners with visiting royalty and world-wide excursions on private executive jets. You don't need to be President of the United States or Prime Minister of Canada to have fun. It could, indeed, be far more satisfying to be Mayor of Oshkosh, Wisconsin, or Saltcoats, Saskatchewan. (On the other hand, if you can believe *that* you're probably too gullible to be in politics anyway.)

There is also the consideration that if we are healthy, wealthy and accustomed to being upwardly mobile, we must give way to the realization that what we are thinking of is inevitably a short-term project. We don't have the kind of time required for long-term political ladder-climbing. We must therefore temper our ambitions and be willing to accept something a little less than the best.

The serious Senior should peer first into what were once genially referred to as "smoke-filled rooms," home of the king-makers and the goodie distributors. That is where the *real* decisions are made. It wasn't Richard Nixon who busted into Watergate. Political pranks are the dream children of advanced thinking and innovative planning by backroom boffins. And if you think *that* was something, you ain't seen nothing yet. Just wait till the new breed of feminists move into Senior territory in force and start looking for new worlds to conquer. The backrooms of the nation are in for a fascinating future — and just think of it — we could be there. Now is the time for us to move in before the big rush is on. Our credentials must be fiscally impeccable if we are to penetrate an affluent riding candidate's backroom. Any hope we might have of influencing his policies or vote is infinitesimal. He and his band of merry supporters are quite happy with things the way they are.

A warmer reception and a more interesting future are more likely to be found in the store-front campaign offices in low rent areas where campaigns are plotted in support of candidates whose successes have been minimal and prospects not much better than dismal. The surroundings may not be that great. There won't be any IBM computers in the corner; the smoke will be from a space heater employed to keep the premises above freezing and beer will replace champagne as the official drink. They need us more than we need them.

Some backrooms, even in today's sophisticated society, are best not entered at all, even out of curiosity. They are hold-overs from an earlier, more individual political age. Their standard equipment consists of baseball bats, brass knuckles, stink bombs, and other rudimentary political persuaders. Newcomers, even elderly ones, will not be welcome there.

Between these "tenderloin" operations, as they came to be known to fiction writers and movie producers, and the more effete political head-quarters of the rich and mighty, a wide variety of backrooms exists. There's sufficient in all to suit even the most discriminating as well as the most adventurous Senior. It's just a case of finding the one that suits us best and then gently moving in. The process is called infiltration.

Our function as infiltrators is to exploit the backrooms so our undoubted expertise may be used to guide the candidate along a course compatible with our special interests. This we must do by making it clear we represent a voting block of overwhelming numbers. We are not there for the purpose of licking stamps or sealing envelopes but have serious goals to pursue. Our initial approach may cause not a ripple, but enthusiasm for our presence will become manifest when we reveal some interesting statistics.

Seniors in both Canada and the United States have demonstrated political clout. The Gray Panthers out of Philadelphia, the city of brotherly (and sisterly) love, are disciplined street fighters and may be counted on to produce a demonstration at the sign of a pension drop. The American Association of Retired Persons has a paid membership of twenty-five million and the most effective lobbying organization in Washington. In Canada, the Federation of Senior Citizens Associations threw a scare in the nation's capital when, in a matter of weeks, they mustered two million demonstrators and petitioners to force the government to back down on a cheese-paring attack on old-age security.

But that's all after the fact. As future backroomers we're thinking not of forcing governments to back down but of putting governments there that will do what we want in the first place. Political pundits, backroom pros and above all candidates who, from the day they are elected, begin worrying about "next time" are accustomed to listening to groups far smaller than ours. Their decisions, however, are influenced far more by the numbers the petitioners represent than the ideals and aspirations they seek to promote.

So, we move in — to have some fun and exercise our fundamental right to promote our interests. Our demands, actually, are few. After all, we're content to let upcoming generations worry about the economy, flying to the moon, war and peace. What we're interested in are simple, basic things like:

- Electing a government that will say NO to mandatory retirement. Let those who want to work, work. Ability, not age, should be the criterion by which all men and women are judged. That's the democratic way.
- Stopping the decline in interest rates. We're not buying real estate any more or educating children or borrowing money to go on world cruises. Our standard of living, mean as it may seem, depends almost entirely on the interest on our life savings. When it goes down, we go down with it.
- Spending more tax dollars on facilities for the Seniors — short hole golf courses, more comfortable park benches, better bars in Senior residences and bigger discounts on travel purchases. And above all: a decent place to live.

That's enough for starters. Every Senior backroomer will have his or her priorities — we need only to remember that nothing's too much for those who have survived sixty-five years of sweat, tears and toil and are still alive and kicking. We've got the numbers, we've got the knowledge and experience and if we're smart we'll get the money. Somewhere a backroom is waiting to welcome the hordes of Seniors marching to the voting booths, flaunting the campaign banner of the nineties: "Senior Power."

I'll be Frank, you be Earnest

Minister of Health & Welfare
House of Commons
Parliament Buildings
Ottawa, Ontario

Sir:

My wife and I thank you immensely for the $2.33 increase in our pensions. Yes, we just can't wait to get our paws on it. In anticipation of such a windfall, next week will be spent oiling my wheelchair and that of my wife, so we can whiz in and out of the stores squandering our money. Man, oh man, this time we'll really be splurging. The hell with paying our taxes!

First off, I'll take my beloved Betty to McDonald's for McNuggets and a cup of coffee. I'll settle for a cheeseburger and some fries.

After feeding our faces, I'll treat her to a bus ride downtown to window-shop all she wants for the rest of the day. I'll still have money left because, now that the warm weather has set in, I no longer have to feed the birds.

On this jubilant note, I'll close here and wish you the best of health (that figures) -- and do keep sending those enriched cheques. I sure need them to maintain my solvency and self-respect. It's a matter of pride, you see.

Yours With Guarded Sincerity,

Frank B. Ricard

FROM ROCKING CHAIR TO COUCH
SENIORS AND MENTAL HEALTH

by Mark Brown

Geriatrics is an area of study concerned with people who are "chronologically enriched." The term geriatrics should not be confused with two similar sounding terms: Geriatricks and Gerihatricks. Geriatricks has to do with older men who spend time with ladies of the evening, while Gerihatricks is a term used to describe three goals scored in a single game by a German hockey player.

Only in recent times has there been much interest in those who have a lot of mileage on their odometers. There was always an assumption that most people, as they grew older, became progressively and finally terminally weird. We know now that this is not the case.

First, let's look at the tell-tale signs of aging. Dr. Methusaleh, the noted golden sage and famous person, has developed a simple survey to help you discover if you are getting older.

Which of the following items apply to you:

- The gleam in your eyes is from the sun hitting your bifocals.
- You decide to procrastinate but never get around to it.

- Your mind makes commitments your body can't keep.
- You turn out the lights for economic rather than romantic reasons.
- You sit in the rocking chair but can't make it go.
- You regret resisting temptations.
- After painting the town red, you need a long rest before applying a second coat.
- Your back goes out more than you do.
- You look forward to a dull evening.
- Your little black book contains only names ending in M.D.
- A dripping faucet causes an uncontrollable bladder urge.
- You have too much room in the house and not enough in the medicine cabinet.

If more than fifty percent of the survey items apply to you, there is cause for concern. If seventy-five percent of the items apply, you should definitely think about retiring.

Retirement is a time when others seem to treat you differently. There are those who respect age only when it's bottled. Seniors are often treated like statues in the park. They are overlooked by people on their way to more important things, and Seniors can end up feeling like they don't matter to anyone. This kind of treatment can lead to laments such as the following:

Old age is golden
I have heard it said
But sometimes I wonder
as I go to bed.
My ears in a drawer
my teeth in a cup,
My eyes on the table
'til I wake up.
'Ere sleep dims my eyes
I say to myself;
Is there anything else
I should lay on the shelf?

Nature may side with the hidden flaw, but it's necessary to keep going and stay mentally healthy. Choosing your battles at this time is important. As one vigorous elder noted:

I don't mind reaching
the unreachable heights . . .
It's just fighting those
unbeatable foes that's a bitch.

The biggest fight of all to stay on your toes may come from within your own family. "Have a seat Grandpa. I'll carry your coffee . . . don't strain yourself." Although it's nice to be pampered once in a while, it can become too easy to let this rest turn to rust — and poor mental health. But remember that insanity is hereditary — you get it from your children!

Frequently, people who are older are referred to as "senile." This term is believed to have originated in one of two places. According to Ripley's *I Don't Believe It But It Must Be True Because It's in a Book*, the term "senile" originated in South Africa when Sir John Smythe, the legendary hunter and name-caller, spotted his befuddled and frequently lost companion, Niehls Loom and exclaimed "See Niehls!" Since this time, the term "senile" has been used to denote someone who is lost in the forest of his own mind. The second origin of the term came to us from an Egyptian papyrus which chronicled the reign of Pharaoh Darryl the Strange. Each day the Pharaoh would walk near the great waters and point saying "See Nile, See Nile." As Egyptians were known to say in regard to the well being of their leader "Tut, Tut."

It has been said that one loses two things with age — memory, and I forget what else. Memory loss and senility are seen as the unholy marriage of aging, but this is far from the truth. Children have to remember only the way home and what time dinner is, but older individuals must recall all kinds of things, such as what numbers will win the lottery, the best buys in the local stores, details of the fishing season, and all the names of their grand- and great-grandchildren. Cicero, who noted that the last thing a man forgets is where he left his money, never dreamed of the idea of cheques or credit cards. Is it any wonder that people who are chronologically enriched may have a little difficulty with memory.

Many young people look upon Seniors as asexual. In fact they usually see their parents as asexual. Or as one teenager exclaimed in regard to his parents and sex: "My father maybe, but my mother never!" When it comes to sex, there is some truth in the adage "use it or lose it." One seventy-four-year-old man, when he was asked if he still liked sex, said " Yes. Just because I can't run around the park ten times like I did when I was eighteen, doesn't mean I don't enjoy meandering through the garden smelling the flowers!" Another gentleman with frost on his roof noted that yes, there was still fire in his furnace. When asked if sex changed with age, he replied, "Yes, it takes longer — but it's time well spent."

Now we must turn to the darker side of mental health and the elderly. The age of the problem — not the age of the patient — is the key here. Some psychiatrists are all too quick to judge the older person. They must be reminded of that ancient and time honored dictum: "Let he who is without neurosis cast the first diagnosis."

Naturally older people must be evaluated to assure that they get any treatment they might need. While this can be done by a variety of mental health specialists, the psychologist is uniquely qualified. These noodle checkers are skilled professionals who can count marbles through a variety of sophisticated tests and interviews. Results are then used to assist Seniors in adapting to life's changes.

In the short space available in this article only a sample of these questions can be presented. The most common type of test used is the personality inventory. These inventories are designed to tell the noodle checker something about how you deal with situations. Generally you are asked to check T for true and F for false as each item applies. A sample set of statements follows. Which of these questions are true for you:

- I sometimes feel that the years have slipped from my hands like tiny goldfish.
- Most people lack the proper balance between hate and malice.
- I would like to draw other people's children (and quarter them).
- I do most of my reading on the toilet.
- My teeth sometimes leave my body.
- A wide necktie is a sign of tasteless relatives.
- Sometimes I am unable to prevent clear thoughts from entering my mind.

- Sometimes I have difficulty remembering what I have done after watching eight hours of television.
- Most people aren't as old as they think they are.

After this evaluation, you will be presented at a case conference where your history, behaviour and the rest of your tests will be exposed to others and then harmoniously blended into a plan of needed treatment.

Treatment can consist of a variety of methods. As mentioned above, psychotherapy can be very useful as can be medications. Increasingly, however, efforts to keep elders mentally healthy have focused on creating community based activities and programs. These programs are low cost and provide a unique opportunity for continued learning and socializing. A list of typical courses are included here:

Workshops

I. Self-Improvement

A. Creative Suffering
B. Overcoming Prejudice of Mind

II. Health and Fitness

A. High-Fibre Living
B. Guilt Without Sex

These workshops are clear proof that age is largely a case of mind over matter — if you don't mind it doesn't matter. Stay involved, be vigorous and continue to work on something that matters to you. That way you can live long enough to be a nuisance to your company's pension plan, to spend your children's inheritance, and to enjoy life. Now that's geriatric mental health!

REINVENTING
THE SENIOR

by Robert Ludwig

The aging process is loaded with malarky. Age has plusses that often outweigh the minuses. At milestone sixty-five a person has learned to cope with emotional cross-currents, bad poker hands and political turmoil. The mature person has dropped many illusions and, contrary to popular junior opinion, the Senior can learn new tricks. The elder may, in fact, be more sensitive to new ideas.

One can hit a high IQ score when still very young, but sagacity and wisdom come slowly. A high IQ means that you can understand that E equals mc^2. Wisdom means that you can dissect a political speech and correctly evaluate the fool who made it.

The number of Seniors is constantly increasing, so it's time that juniors dropped their distorted image of their elders. More important — it's time to develop and exploit Seniors' rich backgrounds. But will junior members of our community listen to their elders? And who will they consider Senior? A fifteen-year-old sees a twenty-fiver as elderly. To the twenty-five-year old, fifty years of age makes you the Ancient Mariner, while the fiftyish one regards the seventy type as an ancestor.

I CALL IT: 'UNTAPPED RESOURCE'...

Cartoon by Graham Harrop

One role assumed by those who have an age-edge is that of advice dispenser. Often the advice given is sound, but too many Seniors nag and bore, having little skill in communication. Then again, juniors may have such poor intake valves that every capsule of wisdom is rejected. This fact shows up in the dreary mistake-repeating and wheel-reinvention seen in every generation. A greater effort is needed to cut down wisdom rejection and mistake remaking. To this end some well pondered thinking is presented herewith.

Any group of Seniors can present a cross-section of world experience, accumulated smarts drawn from deep memories. Picture if you will, a group of Seniors at a table with beer and cheese. Although they might bore the hell out of each other, the same dithering ancients can and will produce profound thinking when led by a chairperson working in a pre-set direction.

This fact suggests the value of Seniors working in panels to evaluate problems in merchandising, industrial relations, political and social areas. Store managers could use Seniors panels to avoid clumsy promotional work, the advice of sycophants and close relations can be balanced by objective observation.

Seniors panels would be especially useful to scrutinize and evaluate candidates for public office. Ego trippers and low-talent hopefuls now cluttering councils and legislatures would be screened out, thus improving the calibre of our elected people. Who wouldn't profit from that process? Much cheaper than primaries, too!

Also demanding Senior-panel scrutiny is the swamp of badly written broadcast commercials. Ad agency execs hate to admit that their stuff has a high redundancy quotient; but even the best of the thirty to sixty second efforts will emit an odor after a few exposures. Panels of Seniors could monitor many hours of commercials, working with a rating sheet to arrive at redundancy quotients. Such panels could also recognize good commercial work, helping advertisers to treat their customers with respect.

There is a varient in Seniors-panel operations that should be mentioned, even though purely academic in projection. In ancient Persia (circa 600 BC) council members used a built-in second thought technique in their deliberations. Before mulling a question of import the council members got drunk. In that state they arrived at positions that were recorded by the scribes, who, of course, remained sober. Next day, or maybe a week later with all the members recovered, their sauce-soaked thinking was read back to them. If they still liked their decisions, they were adopted, and if not they could be reversed.

Perhaps we should see panels of decision reviewers who can work in either state for a suitable fee. Seniors groups including older service club members could serve the community in this demanding way.

Seniors evaluation panels should not be confused with the least effective form of political group, namely the think tank. Such tanks are often staffed by people who haven't sprung an idea in a lifetime, but who are suddenly expected to be creative. Seniors panels could perhaps operate more like the brainstorm circles that were widely used during the 1950s and 1960s. They could be effective when used with some imagination and organization. They are still seen in West Germany, Switzerland and Japan.

The big trick in brainstorming is to alter and rearrange viewpoints by including objectivity. The chairperson has to block the resistance to new ideas and personal bias. Much preparation is needed for brainstorming sessions. There is often a series of meetings, which are taped and replayed to expose the most negative members, who may be dropped forthwith.

The Seniors panel is suggested as a way to exploit the wisdom of those who have accumulated much cunning. Other ideas are waiting to emerge. Let's stimulate and activate!

DUMB LIKE A FOX
HOW TO MAKE
PREJUDICE WORK FOR YOU

by Blaine McTavish

The young perceive Seniors generally as being a harmless bunch, if perhaps overly fond of bingo and department store basements. Beyond their fabled skills at porch sitting and whittling, not much is expected of them.

Occasionally, they are entrusted with children, cats and houses for the duration of someone's vacation, and there is a certain pressure to remember everyone's birthday.

Outside of the immediate family (and sometimes within it) Seniors are often treated solicitously; spoken to like children and catered to like lunatics. Though you may have been the CEO of a large corporation and an avid mountain climber, your niece describes you as "sixty-nine and he *still* gets up by himself. Totally amazing. I hope I have that much energy when I'm, you know, out of it."

Prejudices are not easily put aside and it's a good guess that these perceptions will be with us for some time. The trick is to use this prejudice to your advantage.

You and Your Will

In Chinese culture, elders are revered. In Western culture, much the same effect can be achieved by casually and frequently alluding to your will. The fact that you had it drawn up when you were thirty-two, and that you are still healthier than anyone in the family, doesn't weaken your position.

Next time you leave a room, excuse yourself by saying something like, "Night folks, I think I'll just go upstairs and tinker with my will." The next morning a subtle yet unmistakable change will have occurred. Nephews will want to go out and toss the old pigskin around. Nieces will want to hear stories about the war, despite the fact that you spent the war in Plum Coolie, somewhere on the prairies, with flat feet. A cascade of Viyella shirts will descend on you from everyone, who, to an inheritor, just happened to see them and couldn't help thinking of you.

Breaking the Law

As a citizen, you are expected to adhere to the laws of the land. As a Senior, that expectation can be negotiated. For minor traffic violations, you can almost be assured of immunity by pulling a Helen Hayes routine. Ms. Hayes has made her living of late by appearing in films as the sweetly doddering old person who gets away with murder by smiling and behaving like everyone's dotty aunt.

When stopped by a policeman who would like to know why you were speeding, aren't wearing a seatbelt, and don't have a valid driver's license, point out that the officer looks a bit like your late husband (this can still work if your husband is in the front seat with you, but can get tricky). Smile, act a little confused and mention that your son hasn't written since 1963. The officer can pretty well be counted upon to respond with a mild warning and to leave with a vague feeling of guilt.

Guilt is the operative emotion when dealing with the general public. Many people feel some measure of guilt on the subject of Seniors, usually stemming from infrequent calls to their own parents or that careless vote they cast for a government that wants to de-index pensions.

Senility: When to Use it

When boarding an airplane, it is always best to avoid the crush of business people filling the aisles and bumping one another with hard cornered briefcases. When the announcement for "passengers requiring boarding assistance" is made, assume a slumped posture and amble to the gate, looking saintly. If you have a flair for the dramatic and a certain capacity for mischief this persona can be used to get just about anything. You can take someone's seat at the opera, enter a movie line-up three from the front, convince bus drivers to drop you at your door and persuade grocery clerks to carry your bags to your apartment. It is a good idea, though, not to be caught playing a killer game of tennis in a neighbourhood where you have been working this scam.

When you meet someone at a party who says "Hi, I'm Herb. I'm in shoelaces — the marketing end," it may be time to plead senility. Before Herb can give you a fiscal breakdown of the third-quarter profit, launch into a vague, paralyzingly meaningless anecdote of your own: "Mildred's knees always gave her trouble in the winter months . . . winter of '24, first we noticed anything . . ." A patented senile anecdote is an effective weapon in the right hands and will get rid of most bores. A nice touch is to weave a subplot into your story that has no relation whatever to the subject. For example, randomly inject a description of the movie *Old Yeller* into the mounting suspense of Mildred's knees. When the listener questions the connection between the movie and Mildred, smile blankly and reply, "Mildred who?"

Dispensing Wisdom for Fun and Profit

One of the bright spots of old age is the tie-in with wisdom. All famous wise people (Solomon, Confucious, etc.) met the challenge of dispensing wisdom by handing out enigmatic advice in the form of catchy aphorisms: "Eat to live, do not live to eat" — this from smug fat Ben Franklin. As a living embodiment of wisdom, you are allowed to draw things out a little. When asked for business advice, present an aimless, but related parable: "I'll tell you the same thing I told old Tom Buckner. Asked me if he should invest in plastics (pause). It was 1962. I said to him . . . I said, 'Tom, you stay up with the owls, you can't expect to fly with the eagles' (wry chuckle) but do you think he'd listen?"

For reasons not completely understood, folk wisdom works best. The idea that rural folk have had first-hand experience with the verities of nature has made them oracles to a new generation of urban pinheads. Even preposterous lies will be accepted as oblique wisdom if delivered in the right tone: "Oh, it would be about forty years ago now that them locusts came and et up Uncle Newt . . . Course I warned 'im not to sleep out there in the wheat field . . . Well, laziness pays the devil's dividend, I always say."

If you dispense advice, there is a good chance you will eventually get appointed to the Senate. Simply stated, the Senate is retirement without the responsibility. As a Senator you will be paid about $60,000 a year to dispense wisdom to an unheeding government.

If the Senate is full, you still have a shot at being a talk show regular, as long as you claim to be a one-hundred-year-old man who believes that the space program is a Hollywood hoax.

Financial Planning

Self-help books that boast titles like *Making A Million Overnight* and *Rags to Riches In Thirty Days* have frequented the best-seller lists for for years now. I had always assumed that these books would be full of solid investment strategies and presbyterian maxims like "watch your pennies and the dollars will take care of themselves." I was surprised, then, to learn that many of these books promote practices that are sneaky, unethical and essentially fraudulent.

Among the techniques for making a fortune that caught my eye were methods of delaying the payment of anything by cheque. The book advocated a practice of leaving out essential components — such as your signature — when mailing in payment. The idea being that it takes months for the cheque to come back, at which point you sign it and list the year as 1968, claiming dyslexia. These methods are predicated on the notion that you can plead honest forgetfulness and indefinitely stall all your creditors.

Seniors are credited with a capacity for forgetfulness that shouldn't be ignored. You may want to consider that added touch of making everything you write completely illegible, using a shaky horizontal line instead of actual letters and numbers.

Moral Outrage: Using it for Personal Gain

Society depends upon Seniors for outbursts of moral outrage, which, given the times, is a big responsibility. Why provide this service for free? The next time you go to an X-rated movie, ask for your money back, even if you liked the film. Should the management point out that warnings of sex and violence were plainly posted, adopt guerilla tactics. Stand outside the theatre and introduce yourself to those arriving for the next showing: "Hello dear, I was at the 7 o'clock show. I left in the middle of the cannibalism scene. I asked for my money back but the manager told me to get lost or he'd break my arm." This technique usually gets results fairly quickly.

Thousands of years ago, a Senior was anyone who made it past thirty. Certain gains have been made since then that have enabled thirty-year-olds to remain the cultural equivalent of teenagers. The result of this trend towards youth is that Seniors have been relegated to a status slightly below that of home computers. A move to change this perception is afoot, but if you can't change the public's perception, you may as well take them for what you can get. Or go the well-trodden route of willing everything to your cat.

Seniors' Business Cards

Cash in on over sixty-five years of experience!

SeniorLoto, Inc.
6/65
Instant Bingo

1-800-555-7777

6/65

HARRY HOUDINI
MAGICIAN
Magic Lessons
Students must bring their own pension cheques,
grocery bills and taxes.

h.h.

GOLDEN CATERING SERVICES
Food like Grandma used to make it
— cause she still does

EMERITUS
MANAGEMENT CONSULTANTS

There isn't a problem we can't solve.

EMC

THE BLUE RINSE
MODELLING AGENCY

Specializing in Models Over Sixty

555-6060

MARRIAGE COUNSELLOR
Zsa Zsa Gabor, Consultant

ASSERTIONS OF A FLAPPER

by Claire Richardson

Ladies, no matter how we look at it we who cut our teeth on the Charleston and the Black Bottom, we gems of the western world are getting the shaft. Right? Who has decreed that at sixty-five we have one foot in the grave and the other on a banana skin and that we have the wit and wisdom of your average politician — and God knows, they are average at best, aren't they?

Yesterday a Senior citizen newspaper was flung at my door. I glanced at the pictures of ladies knitting afghans and read the two hundred ways I could murder a pound of ground beef and still have it taste of old sneakers before I roared, "What in the name of God is this thing doing here?" I say "roared" with some attempt at honesty. There are women of my age (seventy-two) whose voices caress like soft breezes in temple bells. My dulcet tones would have put King Henry's rallying of the troops at Harfleur to shame. I don't need this paper. I have never felt older than thirty-two and shall continue to feel this way until, of my own accord, I decide to join the feathered choir, where I shall seek out Robert Browning and demand to know how he had the gall to write "grow old with me, the best is yet to be." Browning, of course, was born old. That crummy beard and gethsemanic glance could never have lured me behind the woodshed. As for bed — forget it! No wonder Elizabeth languished on that couch. Why didn't she get up, search for a new location and try the horizontal gavotte with a man with a gleam in his eye.

The most infuriating aspect of growing older is that the young don't understand your jokes. Be prepared to be thought senile. Try it out in your favourite liquor store. Ask the manager what he has in stock today guaranteed not to poison you and watch his knuckles go white. He will do the four-minute mile in two seconds.

Recently, while I was sitting in a hospital wheelchair, bandaged foot aloft, looking like Henry VIII with gout, a charming young intern asked if I was waiting for someone. "Tom Selleck," I said, glancing at my watch. "You don't suppose he has stood me up do you?" he did a double take and almost walked into the ladies' washroom. He was followed by another young intern — all blue eyes, blond hair and smiles — who screwed up his mouth in a gesture of sympathy at my predicament. "Is there anything I can do for you?" he asked. "How about the next waltz," I said. He beat his fist on the wall, laughed outright, and I envied all the lovely girls he must have been dating. Youth is too good for the young to appreciate, but this sweetheart had it all together. He wheeled me to the lobby door where my daughter was waiting, and helped me into the car — an orange sports Camaro. "Sharp car," he said to her, "very nice." "It's Mother's," she said, "do you believe it — she of the lead foot!" As we pulled away he gave me a wink and wave, chuckling his way back to the hospital. I blew him a kiss. "How do you meet these gorgeous men?" asked my daughter. "Charm," I told her. "I'm lousy with it."

I'm convinced we one-time flappers have allowed ourselves to be shafted for fear of opening our mouths or making a scene. You don't need to act like Ghengis Khan on an off day to get service.

Are you putting up with the crap the banks are handing out? With two tellers on duty, I found myself the thirtieth person in a line-up, all of us were expected to wait like a bunch of yo-yos. I asked a passing employee where the manager was, and was told he was with the bank examiner and could not be disturbed today. "I don't care if he is with God," I said. "I help to pay his salary. Where is his office please?" I banged smartly on his door with the knob of my cane, and the door opened half an inch to expose an indignant eye. Let me say here, I am not your petite size three; I am your tall, winsome size forty-four — Angelo Mosca in drag. On this day I was wearing a scarlet suit with a red, white and blue scarf: Britannia on the warpath.

However, I gave him my simpering "Scarlett O'Hara lunching with the Tarlton twins" smile, and asked if he would kindly cash my cheque, as I could not stand as long as the queue demanded. He explained that the bank assured clients of being helped by a teller within four minutes of waiting. I offered to give him the cheque if he would change places with client twenty-nine. The examiner leaned forward to watch, needing his handkerchief rather quickly. Eyeball to eyeball we stuck it out till, furious and graceful as a cow with a musket, the manager loped across the bank to an inner sanctum, and then returned with my money. I offered a white-gloved hand, and thanked him for his courtesy, but I didn't bother to genuflect.

My grandson, Simon, a true child of his generation, watched the proceedings and then yelled, "Nana, can we go to McDonald's now?" "Yes," I said, "but it's your treat." He laughed. So did Nana.

The Detroit Rubber Company
The Renaissance Center
Detroit, Michigan

RE: <u>The bursting of your hot-water bottles</u>

Sirs:

   I'm an extremely patient person, but this is the third
time that one of your incontinent sieves has inundated
my bed. The first time was when I was prostrate with a
slipped disc; the second time, a bleeding ulcer; and the
third time was when I was trying to get over a one-thou-
sand-horsepower hangover. To add to my woes, my wife
accuses me of having an irritated bladder, loose kidneys and playing Pee in the Ocean. It's a good thing I
wasn't scalded, because I'm afraid you people might have
found yourselves in hot water.

   Is there no way that you can improve the manufacture
of these ersatz, leaky hot-water bags? Invariably, at
one-thirty in the morning, the damn thing bursts. Does
this mean that I have to don a scuba-diving suit every
time I get into bed? I think in future I shall find it
much safer, and even funnier, if I simply fill up an
ordinary paper bag with hot water. That way, even if it
splits open, I shall at least have the satisfaction of
hearing it bang.

   I am returning your defective product today, as the
printing on the package proclaims a three-year guarantee.
I would be most appreciative if, instead, you would send
me a refund.

               Yours Very Truly,

                  Frank B. Ricard

So

YOU'RE RETIRED, AND ON A FIXED PENSION. REDUCED INCOME NEEDN'T CLIP YOUR WINGS. HERE'S HOW TO TAKE THAT PENSION CHEQUE AND **REALLY** MAKE IT **GO SOMEWHERE !!**

turn ➜

by Tony Jenkins

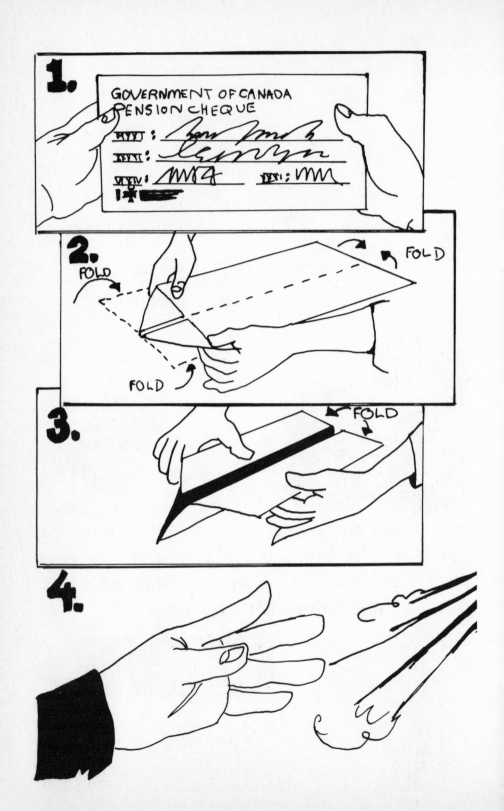

LAUGHTER:
THE BEST MEDICINE

by John F. Moriarty
and Ann L. Nazzaro

A man went to his doctor who told him "You have only three weeks to live." "But Doc," said the man, "I don't think I can pay you in three weeks." The doctor shrugged. "Okay," he said, "I'll give you six weeks."

For various reasons, I've been in and out of the hospital for what seems like a hundred times in the last few years. I've had just about every test known to medical science. I've seen every kind of doctor they've ever invented. I've been in public hospitals, private hospitals, teaching hospitals, Catholic hospitals, Jewish hospitals, big hospitals, small hospitals — you name it — and they all remember me fondly.

One thing I've learned — survival in a modern hospital isn't always easy. One time I was in for a series of blood tests. There I was, just sitting in my room watching "General Hospital" on TV when in comes this nurse in a mask and surgical gown. "Don't worry," she said, "we'll have that new heart in and ticking like a clock in no time." Whoops! Wrong room.

Another time I was in a big teaching hospital for a few days, and my doctor was this fat young intern who had the worst case of gas since the Hindenberg. I mean, I don't like to complain, but when this kid let a good one fly, he set off the smoke detector.

One other time I was awakened at three in the morning by a sheet being pulled over my face. Naturally, I pushed it off. When I did, I saw a swarthy, white-coated orderly who exclaimed something in a language I couldn't place and then said, "Hey, man, *you're* not dead." Wrong room again.

I could go on and on, but the point I want to make is this — although it is the most up-to-date and sophisticated health care facility in history, the modern hospital is a very intimidating and complicated place.

Most people don't know how to survive a hospital stay, what to bring, how to cope with boredom and depression, how to deal with doctors and nurses, and most of all, how to bribe an orderly. The first time I went into the hospital, I was bored, hungry, anxious, and uncomfortable almost all the time. Not any more.

Through the years, I've become an expert. Now, when I go into any hospital, I get first-class treatment. My meals are on time, my nurses are courteous and answer my call button promptly, nobody misplaces my menu or misfiles my tests, and everybody remembers my name. Anybody can achieve this, but most folks don't know how.

A hospital is a busy place. Everybody seems to have something important to do all the time. It's easy to get the feeling that they are too busy to talk to you — and once you lose your spirit, they've got you.

You can tell by how the nurse looks at you that she's thinking, "This one won't be a problem." Maybe you've already seen that look once or twice in your life. Or, maybe you're sitting in a hospital bed and getting that look right now. Don't panic. Help is here. It doesn't *have* to be that bad.

Getting Respect

Life is a jungle. So is a hospital. Medical staff are like animals. There are big animals — like the majestic Chief of Surgery and the great shaggy Head of Nursing. And, there are small ones — like the lowly burrowing orderly, or the timid nurse's aide. The law of the jungle prevails. In order to survive, you must convince the other animals that you are too dangerous to mess around with.

Most people think that a good relationship with the shift nurses is all you need. This is just not true. "The squabbles of the prairie dog go unnoticed by the Buffalo" — African proverb.

In order to thrive in the hospital, you must acquire the proper reputation with *every* level of the staff. There are several ways to do this and several people you must be sure to impress.

We'll start with the doctor. The first thing to remember about doctors is that they deal constantly with life and death situations. Because of this, a doctor may be prone to think of himself as a sort of God. Let him know he isn't.

How? Simple. Doctors respect the law. To insure proper respect and attention, find ways, when talking with your doctor, to mention the word "lawsuit" at least a couple of times. For example, say such things as, "My wife just won her lawsuit against the president of the local teamsters union," or another good thing to do is to get him to think that you are close friends with a lawyer. Say, "Yes, my daughter is completely devoted to me. But she isn't coming to see me today because she's prosecuting a big malpractice suit."

These tactics work amazingly well. Within three days, interns will be bringing friends in to point you out so that nobody makes a mistake with *you*.

But that's just the doctors. How do you impress everybody else? It's easy. Hire an actor to come in and play your devoted, crazy-with-anxiety son. You won't spend much. Ninety-five percent of all actors are unemployed — they work cheap. He doesn't have to be a very good actor. In fact, the worse the better, as long as he's *big*.

He should come in and say in a loud voice, "My father is uncomfortable and his water pitcher is empty. Somebody better start doing something *right now*, or I'm going to throw that chair through this window and take my father out of here, and I'll knock down anyone who tries to stop me."

Have him accost the Head Nurse with, "You've got this whole big building full of people and machinery, and you can't even get an old man a glass of water." He should continue to talk with her about it for at least five minutes after she promises to personally see to it that the situation will never happen again.

After the actor departs — with an appropriately theatrical exit — talk to everyone about him like this: "Yes, yes . . . Mongo, my son, he loves me but he's got such a temper, sometimes it's hard to hold him back. Well, at least Jeff, my other son, is overseas. He's the violent one. I never thought *he'd* be the one that went to law school."

Getting Along with Roommates

When you pack for the hospital, pack two small items — just in case; a small, loud transistor radio and a set of wax earplugs — so you don't have to listen to it.

Unless you are one of the extremely rich or have won a hospital bed in a lottery, one or more roommates will be another of the inevitabilities of your hospital stay.

Roommates come complete with their own problems and concerns, and tend to show a certain amount of indifference to your wants, needs, or wishes. Roommates have family members and friends who are freely admitted to your room at all hours of the day or night and demonstrate disregard for visiting hours and illness. These are people who you would never allow into your home, city, or perhaps even country. These ne'er-do-wells make noise like they are sacrificing bagpipes at the foot of your bed, and say the stupidest things to try to cheer up your roommate, such as:

- Don't be depressed about the leg, it's not like you don't have another.

- At least they have a priest on call here.
- What's wrong with your roommate, she looks terrible.

The key to controlling your roommate's visitors is your roommate. If you brought the radio and earplugs, you're all set. I suggest tuning to either an opera or a rock concert, turning up the volume, and then negotiating a truce. If nothing else works, you can get revenge by bribing an orderly to give your roommate daily enemas.

Lab Tests

Lab tests are an inevitable part of a stay in any hospital. In case you've never had one, the typical lab test goes something like this. You are woken up at four in the morning and, wearing only your hospital gown, you are wheeled into a cold basement room filled with humming machinery. Here they give you a barium enema. They shave your head and paint half of it with orange dye. Meanwhile, everyone else puts on heavy shielded clothing and crouches behind a thick lead barrier.

Coping with the Results of Lab Tests

Don't get excited. Don't jump to conclusions. And, don't believe everything you — or they — read. Sometimes names can get mixed up. Finding out what the test is for beforehand can help *you* evaluate the results. If they took X-rays of your foot and the test results say you're going to have twins, it's probably a mistake.

Visitors

The type of visitors you get will depend on why you're in the hospital. If you are in for tests or minor surgery, expect good friends and close relations. If you are in for something more major, you may see a lot of distant relatives — many of whom will inquire in some oblique way about the provisions of your will.

If you haven't seen some of these people in a *very* long time, just pretend you're somebody else. If they recognize you, pretend you're senile as hell. However, *never* pretend to be senile in the presence of a nurse, doctor, or technician.

Getting Out

When you are leaving the hospital, remember checkout time is six in the morning. If you walk to the exit and they catch you, they will make you walk all the way back to your room and wait for a wheelchair. Tipping the orderly is optional.

One final thing. As you *may* have to return someday, lay a little foundation for respect just in case. Stop by the nurses' station and apologize for the behaviour of Mongo, your "son." "Yes, he's just a bit excitable sometimes. You know I'm *so* glad everything worked out okay — for you folks, I mean."

JEAN TANSLEY'S
BODY REPAIR SHOP

WORK SHEET

Make _____

Model _____

Year _____

Mechanic _____

Qualified Body Expert

MATERIALS REQUIRED

1 New Liver Assembly with thirty-year guarantee
1 New Rectal Unit with Pile Eliminator
1 New Stomach Kit — must be Flat Model with No-Fat Warranty
1 New Dual-Purpose Piston with Certified Lifetime Hardness and
   Daily Performance Features
1 New Permanent Top Hair Unit — Brown, Wavy-type, Slow Growth
   New Back Discs, Non-Slip.

CHECK

Pump — replace worn valves
Bladder and Kidneys — replace with non-deteriorating type if
necessary
Fluid in Main Artery — fill to proper level. Use only blue type.

Send invoice to:
Company name _____

Estimated Cost: $6,000,000

THE TRUTH ABOUT SENIORS

Catherine B. Jensen

"My way of joking is to tell the truth. It's the funniest joke in the world." These are the words of George Bernard Shaw.

It is alarming to detect a sense of powerlessness among the elderly, a sense you can't change anything very much. In a society that worships youth, competitiveness and technology, it seems the most the elderly can hope for is to be tolerated.

We are all responsive, young and old alike, to television's distorted and inaccurate portrayals. With the mature audience watching more television than any other group, it is dangerous to believe what you see is an accurate image of the real world. Crime on television, for example, is ten times greater than in real life.

The facts are that Seniors are not as vulnerable as the media would have us believe. How do we convince someone who is scared to death there is no need to fear, when a barrage of headlines and television images *promulgate* fear?

As members of a rapidly expanding age group, how can we bring about change? Viewers can help change television content by being active, critical viewers. Write letters of complaint or praise to the sponsors. Analyse your own thoughts and deliberate on those of others as to how older people are being portrayed. The *little old lady*, coyly kissing the gas attendant for filling up the tank on the television gas commercial infuriates me. Would anyone really do that do you think — young or old?

Fred Allen once mused, "Television is a kind of radio which lets the people at home see what the studio audience is *not* laughing at."

Help young people form more realistic images of Seniors. Get involved with young folk in whatever way you can. Young people tend to perceive Seniors in unfavourable, negative terms — in large part due to television stereotypes. Even older persons themselves begin to believe the message that anyone over fifty-five is confused, silly, feeble and powerless.

Based on a survey of TV shows it appears that old people are *not* open minded, or adaptable, are *not* bright and alert and are *not* good at getting things done. The television commercials offensive to me show Seniors with migraine headaches, stained dentures and swollen haemorrhoids. Prove these images false! Ailments are not confined to any one age group.

Older people have lived through more technological change than any previous generation in history: automobiles, aeroplanes, telephones, telegraph, radio, television, movies, video, calculators, computers, space shuttles and missiles, advances in every type of surgery, monitoring device and organ transplants. Think of what technology can do for Seniors. The pacemaker has added years to many lives, as have medical and emergency alarm systems. Form citizen advocacy groups. Organize on a national level for clout.

It has been proven that intelligence does not decline with age, and that the ability to learn is not limited to any particular age group. Average healthy Seniors are perfectly capable of performing at the same intellectual level as they did in their thirties. Don't expect, however, to be a genius at sixty, if you were a dud at thirty. Remember the old joke: On the eve of plastic surgery to his hand, following an accident in the woods, the young logger asked his doctor, "Will I be able to play the piano after?" "Of course," the surgeon replied heartily. "Good," the patient beamed, "I've always wanted to be able to play the piano, and never could."

The triumph of the twentieth century is the fact that more individuals are living longer and healthier lives. Women are attaining a greater longevity than men, many into extreme old age. At the bakery where a friend went to pick up a birthday cake for her mother, the clerk exclaimed, "Oh, they've made a mistake, it says, *Happy One-Hundred-and-Seventh Birthday.*" "That's right," said my friend, "and she is as bright as a cricket."

All parties in government need to be advised on Seniors' needs, and who can do this better than Seniors themselves? Ninety percent of Seniors are in the community while only ten percent are in institutions.

At a conference of the Gerontology Association of British Columbia, we discussed how Seniors might respond to this or that situation. Those present were mostly younger folk, professional social workers and gerontologists. Across the hall, members of Seniors' networks were meeting to exchange information and ideas. One elderly gentleman slipped into the room of young professionals and announced, "In the next room you will find a room full of *real, live Seniors.*" There followed an exchange where true anecdotes were garnered to laugh at and to live by. The human race is always hopeful, always pushing towards better things to come.

In the 1940s, when we were young, the leaders seemed to be elderly. William Lyon McKenzie King, at seventy-one, was prime minister. Others in their sixties were in the cabinet. Now that I have reached Senior status, today's government is run by relatively young men and women. There are several members of Parliament in their late twenties and early thirties. The prime minister himself is a young man. How do Seniors get government representatives from another generation to pay attention to them?

Seniors should be running for the House of Commons and the Legislature. There are plenty of dynamic and ingenious Seniors out there, who are articulate in making themselves known with common sense and intelligence. At present it appears that many decisions affecting Seniors are made by government bureaucrats and individuals with little input from *real live* Seniors. That needs to be changed, and *can* be.

... TELL HIM WHERE HE CAN STICK HIS PRODUCT, ALF ...

Cartoon by Graham Harrop

Thirty percent of the electorate are those aged sixty-five and better. To that end we must all get involved in deciding whether there should be new and better organizations, locally and nationally, to anticipate problems, rather than waiting until things happen before we respond.

Single Seniors have special challenges of their own to be addressed. More effective community networks and lobby groups are already forming. An informed public will create a cohesive society. Seniors can be the spark plug.

It seems we have to thank (or curse) the political genius of Otto Von Bismarck, 1815-1898, who dominated the history of nineteenth century Europe, for determining the mandatory retirement age of sixty-five years. Bismarck noted that most of the people died at age sixty-six-and-a-half. In order to score points at the polls, he offered a retirement bonus at age sixty-five. He deduced the commitment would be for one-and-a-half years only. The wiley old fox lived for eighty-three years. It is only now that the sixty-five year retirement age is being questioned.

We have a champion in Dr. Benjamin Spock. Spock, eighty-two, whose books on child care have helped millions of parents, said, at a news conference recently, "The political process must be used to insist society take count of what human beings want, including old people." He cited the practice of forced retirement at age sixty-five as being cruel and unnecessary, and urged that "Employers should have to give employees the right to work as long as they want." An important criteria, of course, is that the individual must be fit for the job.

It is a disservice to Seniors to lump together everyone over sixty-five. The unfairness and stupidity of such generalization is gradually being recognized as wasteful. Leslie Holbrook, in his book, *Making the Most of your Senior Years*, pronounces, "Doing nothing is the most tiresome job because you cannot stop for a rest."

So what can we do to reintegrate with the human race? We have been warned that social reforms that affect only the old and not the rest of society are merely band-aids. We can lobby for new technologies in health care that will enable both young and old to receive medical treatment in their own homes, rather than being institutionalized. Dignity, purpose and independence are our goals in seeking reintegration to society. Seniors could be used as *consumer advisors*, working with manufacturers, engineers and scientists.

Seniors could help with *testing new products* before marketing. Many older people do feel isolated from the mainstream of life. Is this because technologies are developing too rapidly? The human element is the crucial nucleus of all technological development.

John F. Kennedy once stated, "Man is still the most extraordinary computer of all." Let us make the most of our senior years, as an integral part of the human race, positive and hopeful.

You are right, George, the truth *is* the funniest joke in the world!

THE
SPICE OF LIFE

IMPROVING YOUR LOT

by Les Stokes

It's now an accepted fact that the percentage of older people over younger is growing apace, and that the old adage that "life begins at forty" is in need of an upward adjustment. It never was easy, but with today's pressures and that old bogey inflation breathing down our necks, we have had to rely on our own devices to cope with the much-needed home repairs that seem to multiply as soon as one reaches sixty-five. But beware, because do-it-yourself home improvement can almost imperceptibly develop into a socially accepted disease against which immunity and innocuation are virtually unknown.

For those who have managed to keep up with, or stay ahead of, the geriatric Joneses, by owning a drive-around lawn mower, the last word in video equipment or an annually replaced Volvo, these few words are not for such as they. These people will have already completed their courses in Building Construction and Horticulture, and will have attained a diploma in Soft Furnishings and Car Maintenance. These gerontological jobbers have already spent innumerable weekends haunting lumberyards, plant-hire establishments and hardware stores, terrified in case some new tool or innovation has escaped their vigilance. These characters, of course, are extreme pathological cases who, after a succession of nocturnal disturbances from their heavy duty high-speed drills, cause their neighbours to seek alternative accomodation.

My words of advice are addressed more to the majority among us who react somewhat slowly to the gentle prodding of wife and family to do something about the leak in the roof, just above the bed.

In the old days, it would have been a reasonable reaction to phone the local roof repair man. He would have shown up the next morning, completed the job in a couple of hours, and — unlike today — his final account would not have borne too strong a resemblance to the national deficit.

Oh, happy days! Believe it or not, there was once a preponderance of good quality craftsmen, working loyally for their employers, and whose concern was satisfaction and quality of workmanship. But with today's high costs of labour and goods, it has become economically preferable to popularize materials and equipment to appeal to do-it-yourselfers.

There may have been great progress made in the manufacture of tools and in the simplification of operations, but no one can disagree that the old-type craftsmen are thin on the ground. So, the only recourse is to bite the bullet and join the mad throng of do-it-yourselfers.

Getting Started

To start, let's look at those areas where, with a little forethought and planning, we can successfully accomplish those little tasks we are always promising to do something about. First peruse the TV guide for the next few days to assure yourself that events like the World Series, Olympic Games or the PGA Tour are not imminent, and then check that your horoscope agrees that it's time to move Uranus.

A recommended time to begin is at the start of the spring sales, as this gives you a cast-iron reason for keeping away from bargains that you can't afford. Next, stock up with a good supply of cold beer, and you're ready to go. Also, don't forget that most places have building regulations governing a host of items, and to ignore them is to flirt with the possibility of lengthy and expensive legal battles.

Choosing the Right Jobs and Materials

As one grows older, it becomes necessary to modify one's aims on the home improvement front. It goes without saying that the old devil-may-care approach of youth to things like manual concrete mixing has to be tempered, in spite of the hefty life insurance policy you've struggled to maintain all these years. Handling twelve cubic metres of wet concrete for a whole day without a break would have induced a good night's sleep in you at twenty-five, but is more likely to induce sleep of a more permanent nature at sixty-five. Far better to set one's sights on less demanding tasks.

And there's nothing denigrating about asking advice. Heed the old adage that "if anything *can* go wrong, it *will* go wrong." For instance, if you build an outside deck out of chipboard, after the first rain you will have a garden full of Weetabix.

Plumbing the Depths

Stories about plumbers and plumbing have entered the world of legend. In light of this, make a note of the name and phone number of a good local heating and plumbing expert before you start on even the most elementary repair job. Your heating system is, of course, guaranteed to break down in the very coldest weather, when old bones are in need of a little warmth.

On the plus side, plumbing hardware has improved more over the years than any other kind. Now there are plastic products for gutters, wastes and pipes (do *not* use these in hot water locations, or else there will be three drips — water, plastic and you). Portable gas pokers have replaced the old paraffin lamps that our generation were once used to. Like us they have become collectors' items, and you are now more likely to find them in flea markets than in hardware stores.

Finally, do not have a coffee break with friends and leave your poker in an exposed position. The insurance assessors won't give you any marks for having finally decided, along with your cronies, what went wrong at Dieppe.

If I Were a Carpenter

Carpenters at work make it look oh so easy, but practice and skill are needed to get good results. You will need a work bench and quality tools, which you must keep in good shape. When you have built your workbench, always use it, no matter what. No one will forgive the luckless carpenter whose saw has misfired on the Louis XIV repro coffee table. Your bench can also be used for exercise, and will pay dividends. Next, do *not* use your sharpest chisel to open a stubborn can of baked beans — no matter how good they are. Also, if you come across a good adhesive that you can handle easily, stick with it, as it were; avoid all super-glues, since they are best at sticking fingers to coffee pots than anything else.

A wide selection of products especially aimed at preserving wood have found their way onto the shelves of hardware stores. These are available in many colours and have long and extravagant names. Do not let them confuse you. These products have been named to impress professional architects and surveyors, who take a shine to anything called "zyladecoration" on the assumption that its name, coupled with a hellishly expensive price tag, ensures its quality. These products give off powerful and pungent fumes and, if treated in too casual a manner, they can be dangerous. If you have any doubts about what is too strong and what is not, you can invite unwelcome relatives to stay the weekend, and use them in much the same way as canaries were once used to detect gas in underground mines.

Shocking Experiences

As most people know, one of the problems with electricity is that you can neither see nor smell it, but you *can* feel it — and you will certainly know when you have.

The average home has three electrical circuits; a low strength light circuit, a power circuit (for wall outlets), and the stove circuit, which is the most powerful of all. These circuits all need the appropriate fuses and fuse wire in the fuse box, to avoid fires and overloads. A variety of fuse wire should be kept nearby, because it is easy to replace if the need arises. However, when

D-Day arrives, you will generally find that your grandson has used the wire to mend his bicycle. Do not let your frustrations drive you to using hair pins. Call the electrician, and find something else to do.

Power tools can also be a source of great danger, as they are often used without proper grounding. After long use, or after being stored in damp conditions, they will short-circuit. Also, do not drill holes for pictures and mirrors on a line with your socket.

Lastly, do remember to be careful when wiring Christmas tree lights, or else they will unintentionally provide you with a spectacular and unscheduled holiday diversion.

Painting and Decorating

Painting and decorating doesn't have the same macho image as the other do-it-yourself occupations, but the results are usually far more noticable. Preparation is the big thing here, of course. For instance, your brushes should have been kept clean and supple since your last decorating binge, but you will invariably find them in the basement, rock hard and covered in dust.

Also, some thought should be given to dressing for this kind of work. For instance, a cashmere cardigan is not good to make a start in.

Wall-papering is an art mastered by many people, but it is the removing of old paper that is the really hard and untidy work. Sizing the walls will help the hanging process, but the secret lies in the folding of pasted paper, and the use of a jockey — a flat piece of wood — to carry it. I can tell you quite unequivocally that suspending a baton from the window to support the pasted paper does *not* work, nor does recruiting relatives and neighbours to hold brushes under it at a distance.

Beware of visitors who have dropped round and who do not intend to help. They will offer critical comments on your procedures, and will tell you how *they* would have approached the job. This is your best opportunity to undermine those with short tempers, so that you can get out of the holiday you promised to take with them in the time-share flat in Florida.

A Last Word

If, over the years, you have successfully completed a couple of major projects — such as an extra shower stall or an in-ground swimming pool — you will begin to find that you have friends that you previously did not have. They will be forever calling for advice, to borrow expensive tools, or seeking physical assistance in getting their new bath upstairs. Diplomacy is needed here, or you will become a stranger in your own home.

Some folks, after considering the cost of tools, materials and possible damage, think that home repair just isn't worth it. They start looking to buy new properties with all of the features they want already in place. However, whatever you finally decide, bear in mind that it is natural for people to have a hobby of some sort. Winston Churchill just couldn't stop bricklaying, and Adolf Hitler busied himself with painting. As for me, I'm about to patent a walking stick that converts to a long range mastic gun, and I'm seriously considering plans for a work-base that can be quickly and easily fitted to any type of wheelchair — before the neighbours get one first.

GROWING OLD IN STYLE
by Audrey Grayson

Have you looked at a fashion magazine recently? Be honest, now. When did you last flip through one, only to drop it in frustration and dismay? Not because the magazine was unpleasant to look at, mind you, but simply because *you* weren't there.

It would seem that grandmothers wear no clothes. Since all fashion magazines follow the same route, perhaps granny should line up for a spot in a centrefold. Why not? No one wants to clothe her, so she's dressed for the part, you might say. Heaven forbid!

Just look at the situation as it stands. When spring arrives each year, department stores and dress shops burst with colour and lovely new styles to tempt the eager shopper. They begin with baby, who is no longer typecast in pink and blue, and then they move on to display toddlers in the entire spectrum of the rainbow.

Next come the pre-teens, who — I must say — have never had it so good, since they are now allowed to be as fashion conscious as their Moms. That brings us up to the teenagers, whose strong demands are happily met by every retailer in the business. They can be as stylish as they want to be.

Now it's the young woman who has it all her own way. The entire needletrade caters to her slightest whim, turning out garments for every move she makes. Mother doesn't do too badly either, because those in the know recognize that much of Mom's time is spent in the business world and she has places to go and needs the right clothes to wear when she gets there.

But, all of a sudden, fashion stops, just as if life stopped with Mother. Whatever happened to Grandmother? Is she kept in the attic where the need for clothing is practically non-existent?

I admit that some Seniors do find acceptable garments to wear, but only after hours of diligent hunting, and the expenditure of well-honed patience and, heaven forbid, don't put on a few extra pounds. That is when trouble really begins — overweight and sixty. In fact, young salespeople, if they deign to look your way at all, most likely consider you a reject. Chances are, you will never be served again.

They may notice you if you go along to shop with your daughter or a younger friend, but don't expect the salesperson to *talk* to you. She will discuss you with your companion, who, of course, is not senile and may have some idea what you have in mind. But if you are not watchful, the salesperson will pull out some gross garment, made up of a collection of bilious colours and oversize prints. Just right for Granny!

Well, take heart Seniors. All this is going to change. Perhaps not soon enough for some of us, but change it will. And all because of that tremendous wave that washed the land about forty years ago. Remember? Of course you do. The war was over, love was in bloom, and a new phase and phrase were born. Baby Boomers. And with them came the hi-tech market.

Everything imaginable that could be dreamed up for baby, was. These bundles of joy soon trotted off to school and swelled them to the bursting point, spilling youngsters out into so many portables that school yards began to resemble army barracks. The same kids expanded our high schools and then emptied them out just as fast, making scores of buildings obsolete. They went through the universities like a tornado, causing upheaval and change. Did they stop there? Absolutely not. M.B.A. in hand, they invaded the job market and forced Mom and Dad to move on over.

And all the while, keeping right in step with them, were the purveyors of goods, from houses to cars, to big-ticket items to clothing. Baby Boomers, with their strength of numbers and money to burn, had become the richest single group in the country and they are still on the move.

But have you noticed? Something new has been added. Grey hairs are beginning to appear and there is more — much more — to be tucked into jeans. They will keep on fading, but jeans will never fade away. Manufacturers themselves will tell you that Baby Boomers will not give up the garment that has become their security blanket. Knowing this, retailers will expand, re-cut, adjust and do whatever is necessary to cover pot-bellies, sagging hips and swelling thighs.

The Pepsi Generation is slowly but surely moving into the Geritol Brigade, and you can be sure that when it happens in force, Geritol will be sold with class. No doubt a sexy bottle designed to please the eye and excite the palette, will complete the promotion. It might develop into a status symbol and come purse-size, ready to be whipped out at even the most chi-chi gathering, ever ready to keep the Boomies on their feet.

Since this market is so huge, designers of clothes (in fact, designers of *anything*) will go right on catering to them. If the Boomies demand style in their wardrobe, style they will get — at any age. And they *will* demand it; this group will never relinquish the ball they started rolling some forty years ago. So, you see, greying Baby Boomers are catching up to us, and they will blend in with the greying of the land.

You may not wish to wait, of course. So, if you are sixty-five, seventy-five, or whatever, *do not* allow yourself to be bullied into believing that there is no fashion out there for you. You think that way because fashions are not displayed with you in mind. For example, when did you last see a mannequin that was stylish, slightly plump and decidedly sixty?

The clothes are there. Take courage and demand to see them. But you have to know what you are looking for. After all, what is to prevent you from wearing the same smart dress or suit that your daughter wears? (Adjusted to fit, of course!)

When you do shop with a companion, for goodness sake do your own talking. After all, if you can pay for it, you can discuss it. Beware of the salesperson who brings you something that she calls "cute." That's the time to back off. Sixty-fives and over should aim for a look that's classic, elegant and distinguished — but *never* cute.

Well, Grandmother, do you get the picture now? While you are keeping your health and your looks, the Baby Boomers are growing older and closing the gap. In less time than it takes to say no to your daughter's request to borrow your brand new red sweater, marketing executives will see things as they really are and start lining up for a chance to collect the Seniors' dollars.

Meanwhile, Gran, while you are waiting, a tack like this might garner some attention. How about having a large button made for your lapel, and have printed on it these words: I bred a Boomie.

SUNNY VIEW
A Luxury Residence for Seniors

We offer an impressive range of services

- medical specialists on site, including psychiatrists and plastic surgeons

- gourmet chefs trained in Paris

- health spa and tanning coach

- an attorney to attend to emergency will alterations

Application for residence will be forwarded to anyone listed in *Who's Who*, *Debrett's Peerage*, or any telephone directory. A clean bill of health, post graduate degrees, and several million dollars are prerequisite.

Shady Rest
Retirement Home

A perfect home for any Senior living on a limited budget and
with limited expectations

- doctors are only a phone call and seventy-five miles away

- residents may have a hot-plate in their room, or eat at our
  roadside diner

- each room contains a bed, table, rocking chair, cutlery and
  shower stall

For further information, Seniors should contact Norman Bates at
555-1212.

HOME IS WHERE THE HEART IS
LIFE IN A SENIORS' RESIDENCE
by Stuart Richardson

Never, since I was a schoolboy singing "Land of Hope and Glory" in an English school yard on Empire Day, have I known the exhuberance of living one gets to know and love in a Seniors' residence.

My wife and I have two rooms — "His" and "Hers." As is only natural, she gets the better of the deal. She has her own bed, the large TV set, the chesterfield, two easy chairs, a rocking chair, the bookcase and the bathroom.

My room is smaller. Into this small place we squeezed a bed, a bureau, the small black and white TV set and my typewriter on which, one day, I shall create "The Great Canadian Novel." This is not a time to be sitting around without ambition. This is "a time to be up and doing with a heart for any fate."

The bed in my room is a small camp-cot affair that folds up during the day to give me more space. When I was folding it up one morning I noticed a broad arrow and some letters burned on the cross beam. It said "British Army Reject, Crimean War." I took that up immediately with the lady manager and spoke quite sharply. I am very good when in an intransigent mood and said to her, "If it was not good enough for Florence Nightingale it is not good enough for me."

I lost. The manager, who was British, said, "How could you speak so slightingly of one of the most heroic women of the British Empire?" I knew I had lost then and there and slunk back to my room to read Kipling's *Pride and Empire*. There is something that sits hard on a man who realizes he has been beaten by a woman.

They have a lady manager here because there are more ladies than gents. The balance is about the same in every residence of this kind in the country. In our residence the ratio is normal, and so are most of us.

The First Night

The first night that we spent here proved to be very interesting. I am a very nervous person, and when we lived in a house I went through my check pattern before going to bed. Were the front and back doors locked? Had the TV set been left on in the playroom downstairs? Was the fireproof door shut between the garage and the house? Some nights I could not remember if I had checked, and I got out of bed for a re-check.

If there was a creak in the house, I was out of bed like a shot, descending the stairs armed with the assegai my grandfather brought back from the Boer war. Then I would say in a loud voice, "I am fully armed, so make your getaway fast or else you're dead." I picked that up from a John Wayne movie and thought it was quite good. After all, I was never very good with the assegai and am glad I never had to use it.

Here in the residence the silence is absolute. I look up at the ceiling and there is a smoke detector. I look to one side and there is a sprinkler head. If absent mindedly, I smoke a cigar in bed, the spiralling smoke will hit the detector, set off the sprinkler head and sprinkle both me and the cigar right out. We live in a fortress. We are protected. What is more, the services of a nurse are available around the clock.

When I was going to school, I decided that would be the best time of life. There was a joy in finding that the mind had grasped something that had previously eluded it. Then I went to sea, to see the world; on a patched up tramp in a gale in the North Atlantic I thought I was fulfilling life's dream. Then, by a happy happenstance, I came ashore in Canada and this became the best of life. In public relations for a large corporation I travelled the country from one coast to the other with a wonderful open-ended expense account.

The Best

But the time we are living now is by far the best. We are free of worries and free of care and there are no more examinations to swot for. There is no shopping to be done. My wife has no cooking to do, no beds to make or change, and no housework to do. The food here is excellent. Almost every evening there is an event of some kind, and on Sunday there is a P.S.A. meeting (Pleasant Sunday Afternoon). Bingo is on Tuesday evenings and Trivial Pursuit on Thursdays. On other evenings we have slide shows, films (ancient and modern), travel talks, health talks and lots of music in all its forms. I give talks and play appropriate cassettes on the days of St. Andrew, St. Patrick, St. David and St. George.

February 14th is our big day, and this is not just because it happens to be St. Valentine's Day. On that day we have a champagne party and a gourmet dinner. Then we have the entrancing music of violins and the heady taste of wine. It is great. It is joyful. The champagne warms us and the music is delightful. I think back on those other stages of my life and nothing compares to this. This is the way to live. We enjoy every minute of it and go happily back to our halved quarters.

All the Saints Come Marching In

Recently we received word that Sister Felicitas would be conducting an evening service. I'd heard she was good so I went. The service was ecumenical, and we sang some Protestant hymns. At the end of the service the Sister gave a short homily and said, "In this place you should all love each other. Say to one another 'I love you.' It means so much to know that someone loves you. You will come closer together, you will find ties that bind and your lives will be enriched."

She looked at me and I looked back at her. I had a feeling I should say something, so with a twinkle in my eye I said, "I love you." She glided towards me and put a hand on my shoulder. She kissed me on the cheek. "Glory be to God," she said, "He loves me." Now I know what it's like to be blessed by a saint.

Although we are sheltered from the rigours of the outside world we have our high moments and count our blessings. And I wonder what surprise is in store for tomorrow.

SENIORS' CHOICE

7:00

SC Movie
Miracle on 34th Street
A senior citizen takes a
leisurely stroll in the inner
city without getting
mugged.(½ hr)

7:30

SC Over The Hill Street Blues
A blue rinse street gang
establishes a commune on
Hill Street, where they eat
pizza and take Spanish
lessons.

8:30

SC Billy Graham Crusade
An entire hour of viewing
without sex, drugs or
violence.

SC Love Boat
Season Premiere
A retired couple take a
luxury cruise to recapture
what they once had, but
realize that they can't
remember what it was.

SC Amazing Stories
A senior citizen applies for
a professional job with a
good salary and prospects
of promotion, and is hired.

SC NSL Curling
National Seniors' League
Finals from Florida.

8:30

SC **Question Period**
MPs patronize a select group of Seniors, who fail to get satisfactory answers to their incisive questions

8:30

SC **The Second Honeymooners**
A married couple decide to start over by reversing their roles, and the husband is shocked by his wife's chauvinism.

9:30

SC **Seniors' Wrestling**
Suomo Seniors wrestle with some antiquated ideas about their place in society.

9:30

SC **Masterpiece Theatre**
Alistair Cooke introduces "Glitzkrieg" in which the Sequined Historical Theatre Group re-enact the sinking of the *Scharnhörst* in mime.

9:30

SC **Mini Series**
Tomorrow's Not For Sale
Amelia Earhart (Ali McGraw) and Charles Lindbergh (Omar Sharif) conquer the air against a backdrop of Hollywood gossip and political intrigue. Part 1 of 17.

9:30

SC **Price is Right**
People on fixed incomes make improbable guesses at the market value of goods they could never otherwise afford.

10:00

SC **The Spic 'n' Span Show**
Mary Tyler Moore and Dick Van Dyke are a husband and wife scriptwriting team who show how good natured people can still be funny. Guest star Julie Andrews.

10:00

SC **Sixty Minutes**
Harry Houdini shows how he can escape from chains and a locked box in three-quarters of an hour, while Andy Rooney looks on.

10:30

SC **Lorne Greene's Concrete Jungle**
Lorne Greene examines the frail world of urbanites on the brink of extinction.

GOOD ROCKING

by Elizabeth Ruggier

I remember reading, years ago — in *Time* I think it was — a profile of Helen Traubel, a famous lieder and Wagnerian singer of the day of whom it was said she could "belt an aria clean across Times Square." The Square is some fifteen blocks from Carnegie Hall where musical "belting" took place in those pre-Lincoln Centre days. And she did it without electronic assistance or back-up of any kind whatsoever.

Why? Because those were the halcyon days before the electronic industry was sufficiently developed to completely take over the entertainment field.

There are many popular singers today apparently equipped with what used to be known — when applied to Sgt. Majors — as leather lungs, for the power and bellow-range of their voices that they can seemingly project over the heads of crowds of a hundred thousand and more, in the open air. And do the same with comparable numbers in closed-in sports arenas.

But they do so thanks to the ubiquitous microphone, without which they would, nine times out of ten, be heard above a whisper, if at all, in the farthest reaches of an 800-seat theatre.

Of course Helen Traubel wasn't the only one who could do what she did. There were popular entertainers like Ethel Merman, who was no slouch at voice projection, and long-gone Sophie Tucker, whose popular ballad *My Yiddishe Mama* shook the rafters of the largest theatres and concert halls the world then boasted.

But, for all the strings, brass and percussion accompaniments in the world, none of them could produce today's kind of wrenching sound known as Rock'n'Roll.

And there's more. Heavy Metal, Acid Rock, Hard Rock, Romantic Rock, all decibel disasters in their own right. But perhaps it is the span of generations that gets in the way of my inclination to make the effort to understand, appreciate and — conceivably enjoy — this Orwellian-like music scene. But I have always been allergic to massive sound. I mean it makes me physically sick to my stomach.

For that reason I could never cope with Miss Traubel pitted against a full orchestra as, singly and severally they attempted to wrestle Wagner to the ground in any one of his opuses whether magnus or relatively minus!

Then again, I have always opted for the lyrical in music — for the longest time I thought that was what music was all about — and consequently had as much trouble with atonalists like Schoenberg, or dare I say it, Bela Bartok. I would never voluntarily attend concerts of their work. I simply couldn't.

But one thing they had in common; you could hear — if you did not have a weak stomach like me and could afford to listen — every note, every phrase of music, every nuance. You were aware of structure behind the sound. There was no music that I know of with the exception, perhaps of Ravel's *Bolero*, that relied on a single beat or brief phrase; no lyrics that consisted of a single word or, at best three or four that chased each other endlessly up the crescendos and down the falling scales as is the case today.

Where does one go now to savour the cool perceptive and sophisticated lyrics of say, a Noel Coward, Cole Porter or any one of half a dozen more like them, save to a Stephen Sondheim, the last, it seems of a dying breed.

Or for that matter find a female vocalist of the power and intensity of an Edith Piaf, who made the passionate songs she sang her own, without a single snap of the fingers, bend at the knee or strident movement on the darkened stage where the spotlight always found her.

Today's vocalists, male as well as female, must bolster their "talents" with gobs of dry-ice-generated mists, hairdos of the shock-headed-Peter variety and even more so. They must contort face as well as figure, stretch and stride as far as the cord on the flat electric guitar, at whose strings they tear convulsively, will permit them. Even a singer *with* a voice like Tina Turner must don her witches' wig and strut her frenzied *Private Dancer* plastic passion stuff if she is to earn a living, much less "make it" in her chosen profession today.

When it comes right down to it we are all a product of our time and for each of us *our* time was, or is the best. But that leaves out the timeless ones.

It leaves out a great body of popular music of, let us say, the last fifty years, with titles too numerous to mention, that simply refuses to fade away and doesn't even show its age as we poor mortals do!

With the exception of the Beatles, and maybe the Rolling Stones, will the Madonnas, the Princes, and the Boy Georges be found down memory lane? Michael what's-his-name is already half forgotten.

It will be a wonderously quiet world without even the cacophony of human intercourse — *verbal* communications that is! — because without hearing, speech will lapse and sign language will take its place. Old 'uns like us probably won't be around to enjoy it.

Meanwhile, for those whose "thing" it is, "Good Rocking Tonight" as they say on the CBC. For the rest of us, The Peace that Passeth Electronic Understanding.

I'll be Frank,
you be Earnest

The Editor
American Seniors Magazine
215 Pasadena Blvd.
Burbank, California 90802

Sir:

    I may never get to live as young as George Burns.
But, at 70, I manage to keep my feet out of the cemetary
(though not always the hospital, as I occasionally do
enter it for some minor geriatric repairs) by main-
taining a visible attitude of optimism and relaxation.
An instance of this is that I consistently acknowledge
the ubiquitous greeting, "How are you?" with
"I hang loose."

    This world would certainly be a better place to live
in if more people adopted the felicity of the good woman
who said, "When I work, I work hard; when I sit, I sit
loose; and when I think, I go to sleep."

                Yours Drowsily,

                    Frank B. Ricard

WAY DOWN UPON THE SWANEE RIVER

by Patrick Cotter

Stephen Foster had it right one hundred and thirty-five years ago when he wrote the lyrics to the famous song, *Old Folks at Home*. The Swanee River in particular — and Florida in general — is where the old folks stay, American and Canadian.

And why not? By the time the average North American has reached retirement age, he or she has shovelled enough snow to fill a supertanker and shivered enough to shake at least a tooth or two loose.

No matter what your age, when you get to Florida people will tell you that just living there will add ten years to your life. While the official statistics don't warrant quite that much enthusiasm, it is a fact that you'll gain a few extra years if you make Florida your home.

You'll have plenty of time to sit back and watch the next generation sweat it out creating a future for themselves. The best part, aside from it being difficult to catch a chill, is that the younger crowd is making it easier for you to enjoy the fruits of their labour.

You'll also be part of one of the largest crowds in the state. Nearly twenty percent of the population is sixty-five years of age or older. Florida is first among the states in the number of persons over sixty-five living on a fixed income. These figures tend to work in your favour. A considerable amount of time and effort is spent making Florida a more hospitable habitat for Seniors. Numbers speak louder than words in the U.S. economy.

The most difficult thing about moving to Florida, even as a winter resident, may be leaving your family and loved ones behind. Don't fret over-much about that. They'll be down to visit — and stay, and stay and stay — if you let them.

You may also find it hard to choose a spot to roost. Just as Paris is not France (and Toronto not Ontario), Miami and its reputation for crime, is not Florida. The best thing might be to take an extended tour of the state and see what suits your fancy.

Florida is peppered with developments devoted exclusively to Seniors, but your choices for the way you want to live are limited only by your imagination or pocketbook. You can live on a houseboat, a farm or a country club golf course. You can live in a mobile home, a townhouse, a beachfront condo, a downtown highrise or a suburban subdivision.

You must also be warned that hot-headed young folks may fume impatiently at the way Seniors drive — prudently and patiently. Pay them no mind. You've got all the time in the world, and you can do just about everything you did back home all year round — except ski, skate, curl, go snowmobiling, ice fishing or sugaring-off.

Of course, Florida isn't Paradise, even though its mushrooming population might indicate that it's considered the next best thing.

Health care doesn't come cheap, but the care is good if you can afford the price of admission. Again, the numbers dictate that hospitals and medical personnel be able to deal with the needs of Seniors. Check with your provincial or state government and investigate health care insurance options before making the move to a new life in the sun.

In all fairness, it must be pointed out that summers in Florida are long, hot, and humid. As the saying goes, if you can't stand the heat, get out of the kitchen. Visit all those relatives and friends back up north who availed themselves of your hospitality during the winter, and stay as long as they did with you. Florida winters can get chilly, especially in the north, but they're usually nothing more than a couple of nights under the electric blanket.

Of course there is crime in Florida, and politics and taxes. You have survived them elsewhere, so you already know what they're all about and how to avoid the worst of them.

Enjoying yourself seems a lot easier in Florida. Tourism remains the top moneymaker in the state, and you'll finally have the time to do as you please. Florida is dedicated to pleasure, legal and illegal.

After all, which would you prefer; being cooped up on a cold, gray winter morning or coffee on the patio in February, followed by a walk on the beach under the endless summer sky?

SENIORS'
ALL TIME
FAVOURITES

Gene Kelly in *Singin' in the Rain*

Movies

1. *Gone with the Wind*
2. *Ben Hur*
3. *Casablanca*
4. *From Here to Eternity*
5. *A Night At the Opera*
6. *The Three Musketeers*
7. *Singin' in the Rain*
8. *The King and I*
9. *The African Queen*
10. *The Battle of Britain*

TV Shows

1. "The Journal"
2. "The Golden Girls"
3. "The Bill Cosby Show"
4. "I Love Lucy"
5. "Sixty Minutes"
6. "Murder She Wrote"
7. "Dick Van Dyke Show"
8. "The Honeymooners"
9. "The Price is Right"
10. "The Fifth Estate"

Songs	Books
1. "Stardust"	1. *Pride and Prejudice*
2. "We'll Meet Again"	2. *David Copperfield*
3. "Tea for Two"	3. *Treasure Island*
4. "Bring on the Clowns"	4. *Little Women*
5. "White Christmas"	5. *Iacocca: An Autobiography*
6. "My Blue Heaven"	6. *Jane Eyre*
7. "In the Mood"	7. *The Catcher in the Rye*
8. "Danny Boy"	8. *Robinson Crusoe*
9. "Over the Rainbow"	9. *For Whom the Bell Tolls*
10. "Amazing Grace"	10. *The Comedians*

Most Important Historical Figures

1. Winston Churchill
2. Adolf Hitler
3. Mahatma Ghandi
4. Martin Luther King
5. Albert Einstein
6. John F. Kennedy
7. Henry Ford
8. Joseph Stalin
9. Franklin D. Roosevelt
10. Sister Theresa

They Don't Make Them Like They Used To

1. Cars
2. Clothes
3. Blondes
4. Beer
5. Shoes
6. Nylons
7. Men/Women
8. House calls
9. Shirts with cufflinks
10. Toys (except for Fisher-Price)

THE
WAY WE WERE

THE DIRTY DECADE

by Eric Nicol

Compared to the Dirty Thirties, the depression of the Grungy Eighties was mere ring-around-the-collar. I know, because I came out in the wash of both.

Here I must take care not to lapse into Oldtimer Upmanship — the ploy that Seniors use to downplay the significance of anything that happened in the last half century. The winters were colder, the summers were hotter, the women were sweeter, the books were better bound, and of course the Depression — the *Great* Depression — was more harrowing, more character building, and in many ways more fun than that piddling recession that today's young people snivel about as "hard times."

However, the facts speak for themselves. The safety nets of the welfare state did not exist in the thirties. A jobless person had a free-fall drop, plunging straight down from paid employment into the soup kitchen. The brokers leaping from the ledges of stock-exchange buildings, after the Crash of '29, did so with no expectation of landing gently on the ample bosom

of the department of human resources. There existed no visible boundary between Fat City and Splatville.

I was doubly unfortunate in that the Great Depression hit me during a very sensitive part of my life — the teens. Adolescence is difficult enough, God knows and Abby confirms, even in the palmiest of times. To be baffled by sex *and* R.B. Bennett simultaneously could have ruined me for life. Maybe it did. But there were no school counsellors around in those days, to tell me that I was "special" — i.e., disturbed as hell. So I just got on with growing up rather odd. An only child, I was unable to plead "Brother can you spare a dime?" without approaching strangers.

My family was not one of those impoverished by the thirties. My father, a broker's accountant, could afford to drive a car — a green Essex — though he never considered letting *me* near the wheel. I envied kids too destitute to travel by car because I became car-sick every time my parents went for one of our long motoring trips, which was often. I remember my summer vacations as a series of emergency pit stops along the highway for me.

My mother harboured the theory that my ritual regurgitation might be reduced if I didn't watch the scenery going by. "Eye movement does it," she said. Thereafter on our motoring excursions I sat alone and blindfolded in the back seat, or with my head under a blanket. After the Lindbergh baby kidnapping, it became harder for my parents to drive me around blindfolded, because everyone was alert for child abduction. I had to scrunch down behind the front seat when we stopped for gas. And I was still getting about four upchucks to the gallon.

When I was not holidaying with my parents, my normal method of transportation during the Great Depression was to stand on the back platform of a streetcar. Unlike the later generation of recession teenagers, I felt no shame in using public transit. On the contrary, the back platform of a trolley car was where young men became aware of their sexuality. The compression of bodies in that confined space around the conductor, along with the rocking rhythm of the railed boxcar, produced in me novel sensations that I still feel if someone rings a bell while a woman is standing on my foot.

I had no money for dates, of course. I went right through high school without so much as a sniff of the bobby-socked beauties whose mysterious curves and bumps fascinated as much as they terrified me. Alcohol and tobacco were equally remote possibilities to us children of the lean years. The expensive thrills for which today's youth, however "underprivileged," find the money — rock concerts, albums, stereos — were not anticipated by my main vice: reading. Library books however, did not include *Tom Swift and His Electric Vibrator.*

The highlight of my week was the Saturday matinee at the moviehouse, where Laurel and Hardy got into hilarious scrapes that demonstrated the fickleness of Fate, regardless of whether the nation's chartered banks were the next to step on the banana skin. To earn the two-bits for admission to the palace of pratfalls and morally impeccable westerns, I caddied at the Jericho Golf and Country Club, the poshest links in Vancouver. Because I was a kid on part-time caddying, the pro-shop operator always assigned

me to a ladies' twosome — the vocational equivalent of a fate worse than death.

The ladies — usually doctors' wives — economized by having me carry both sets of clubs for the one fee of seventy-five cents. This freed them to spend the next three hours chatting and looping balls into the rough, where I tottered in pursuit, clubs splaying out of the bag as I stooped to the poison ivy in search of the cowardly Spalding.

To this day I can't pass a golf course without my shoulders twitching. But caddying for rich cheapos during the Great Depression did help to prepare me for World War II — I was glad to salute *any* flag that wasn't placed at the far end of the green.

Medicare? For my generation this consisted of biting on the bullet. I'm sure that my parents would have taken me to the doctor if I had some disorder that justified the expense — cholera, for example. But when my mother accidentally slammed the door on my finger, dislocating it grotesquely, the medical attention consisted of her kissing it to make it well. We weren't into mollycoddling.

Like most other young, thinking victims of the Dirty Decade, I was fiercely socialist in my politics. I would probably have been a communist if Karl Marx had written *Das Kapital* as a western. As it was, I replaced God with Bernard Shaw and joined a group of young radicals who sought to redistribute the nation's wealth by taking wealthy golfers.

The pink wore off. A more lasting effect of the Great Depression on us thousands now old enough to be grandparents, was that it made us mean with money. Oh, man, am I canny! Talk about squeezing a nickel till the beaver craps!

Even now, and despite the arthritis that makes it a neural adventure, I shall pick up a penny from the pavement. Yes, one cent. Show me a graduate of the recent depression who stoops to that. When my young son left home, he didn't bother to take his jar of small change. I've been wrapping the pennies for him, waiting for the right moment to return them to him as a token of frugality.

Because of *my* depression, I didn't get married till I was thirty-five and had saved enough money to buy a house outright — cash on the line. The thirties had taught me to view a mortgage as the work of the Devil in league with the C.P.R. Only in the past few years have I reluctantly accepted the use of a credit card, mostly because writing a cheque is dicey without my glasses.

Conditioned by the biggie of financial barrens, therefore, I cannot understand those who see a job as a tedious episode between school and unemployment benefits. My mind understands the rationale that today's technology has created a chronic unemployment that may well become permanent, but the 1930s part of me screams bloody murder at the layabout elevated to a martyr for the cause of automation.

That is the deep-down grime in my soul, thanks to the Dirty Thirties. Nor will all your tears wash out a line on this face that fortune spurned.

LOST IN WARTIME BRITAIN

by Jack Peach

The sudden transplanting of "right-handed" Canadians in uniform into the blacked-out habitat of the "Limey left-handers" was enough to cause mild panic. It was 1941 and the enemy across the Channel, and all around the tight little crowded islands, was poised ready to strike. As though that was not tension enough, we had to find our own way around the place.

With dismaying frequency our accents fell with an alien clang upon those island ears. An English cadence slyly nurtured at a spy camp near Munich, or born on a sheep station out back of Kalgoorlie, or at a good school in Cochrane sounded just about the same to the good burghers of Torquay, Burnley, or Galashiels. So, without warning, a casual but jolly conversation could be cut off in mid-syllable, giving way to silence as impermeable as granite. And all you had said was, "Shucks, was I ever lost!"

Because the enemy was at the point of launching a seaborne invasion in addition to his nightly air-raiding, all direction signs had been erased from the face of the land. Not a road sign, or a railway station destination board, or a timetable, or a street guide remained for public viewing. London buses and Underground trains were permitted to display route numbers and destinations but once you climbed aboard a No. 30 bus whose order board declared it to be headed for Roehampton, you hadn't a clue where you were along the route, or whether you had arrived there once the big red double-decker lurched to a stop.

So, you asked the conductor "clippie" which way to Kingston Vale. "Orl roit mate," she'd say, leaning confidentially towards you lest an enemy agent might overhear, "You tike the road on the left, there, bear roit at the Bull and Crahn — 'at's a pub, love, foller frou to the end of the laneway and you'll come to a rahnd-abaht. Orlroight? Well, circle the rahnd-abaht, keep left, straight frou to St. Martin's Church an' it's stright dead ahead of yer, Ya cawn't miss it!"

So you followed her directions implicitly and ended up looking a trifle foolish because dead ahead of you was The Swan Inn, complete with closed wooden gates that apparently lead into a courtyard. Nobody to ask, nobody to follow, so the only thing to do was to go in, have a drink to ease your aching feet, and ask the way.

You did not think you looked particularly like a skillfully-trained Nazi in civvies hiding a cunningly-forged passport and food coupon book, but you were treated like one. Because you didn't speak the lingo or know anyone, you were under suspicion in an instant, wishing you were wearing uniform instead of very un-British tweeds! There was much whispering and glancing, nudging and nodding and, as you slurped the top layer of the pint of warm bitter, in strode a remarkably sturdy policeman.

"Well, now, what's all this, then?" he boomed while the entire clutch of locals fell silent, staring open-mouthed, ready to storm in a tight circle as soon as the pinch was made. " 'Ere, 'ere," nudged the law, "May I please see your identification, sir?" You shuffled, scuffled, dug, prodded and probed and, from a pocket it never should have been in, produced your documents, which you timidly proffered toward the blue serge arm with its striped "on duty" cuff.

"Well, well, well," beamed the copper, "A bloody Canadian! Why didn't you say so, sir!" Approvals surged from suddenly dry throats and there followed a gaggle of treating one another to drinks. It was most jolly and you remembered your mother back home in Canada, she being a fan of the old music halls of her girlhood days in England, chanting, "If yer want to know the way, ask a p'liceman!" "Officer," you asked courageously now, "Am I anywhere near Kingston Vale?" " 'S'truth, Canider, you're on it!" "But I didn't come past the Bull and Crown." "Lucky for you," boomed the copper in high glee, "Or they'd of recruited you for the Home Guard would that lot, eh chaps?"

Thus you discovered that it was thoroughly possible to lose your way even with the most explicit instructions. There seldom was doubt as to the centre of any village, town or city. If you were on High Street you had arrived there! Bombing may have flattened the neighbourhood but if someone deaf to your accent happened to let it drop that you were on High Street you knew that it led, however aimlessly, through the ancient heart of the settlement.

Company vehicles with sufficient petrol coupons were permitted to bear their firm's name even though the address and telephone number had been obliterated by slashes of black paint. In search of one particular garrison town that could not be found on an army map, I recall trailing a bouncy

little van that scurried along one of the byways. As I was at the steering wheel of a hulking armour-plated recording truck, it was not easy to keep the little vehicle in sight. I wondered if the owner was careless or cunning for having left the firm's name and its home base emblazoned on the rear doors of the van. It read, "Makers of the Bridal Barm."

The map, for all its excellence as a guide for the defenders of the Heart of Empire, yielded no sign of the location of Bridal Barm. It was not until some time later, following a lot of questioning, that it turned out there was no such place as Bridal Barm, nor was there a firm run by a Mr. Makers. The van, it turned out, was a courier for a manufacturer of, shall we say, virginal yeast culture, or barm, used by brewers of malt liquors! So much for anonymity!

One constant collector of lost souls was the London Passenger Transport Board's network. It had red double-decker buses, single-decker suburban buses in red and in green, trains that had inherited the century-old endless Inner Circle route from ancient steam trains, and the long red Underground trains that, but for the outer limits of their routes, slithered along the lacework of "tubes." They were all carriers, uncannily reliable, that moved thousands of passengers by day and night.

In order to fool the forever-expected enemy, blatant destination in-dicators had been replaced by absurdly demure Underground station markers. Moreover, to protect passengers from flying glass, above or below ground, the carriage windows wore an opaque coating of woven string and, one presumed, isinglass. However, a tape-edged, diamond-shaped peephole did permit one to peer out at the little station names whizzing past as the train slid to a halt.

Frequency of service on all lines was restricted so that riding public transport became an intimate adventure in a standing or sitting position. To keep the crush of passengers in some semblance of flowing streams, the LPTB introduced to its hurrying gas-mask-carrying patrons a dapper little cartoon character drawn in typical, crisp David Langdon style. This small businessman wearing morning jacket, striped trousers, and billycock hat, carrying a "brolly" and packaged gas mask, was named Billy Brown of Lon-don Town. From placards everywhere he addressed passengers who were weary of rationing, nightly air raids, bomb shelter bunks, fire watch and canteen duty. Billy Brown's name was enough to make a tired traveller retch but his smugness was even more sickening. The idea accomplished, in a master-ful way, exactly what the Transport Board wanted it to: to needle the travellers into an awareness of the need for cooperative behaviour to keep the system operating as smoothly as possible under siege of war.

We passengers tended to crowd near bus exits and rear platforms. Billy Brown appeared on placards aboard and at stops, staring with Dutch Uncle persuasiveness, "Kindly move along the bus — and so make room for all of us." Equally often he admonished us, "To crowd the entrance is silly, so, 'Let's all move along!' says Billy."

With the blackout severely enforced, buses with tiny cross-slits as headlights travelled rather blindly, especially in the countryside. It was only prudent to peer intently for the bus, then flail one's arms like a demented semaphore railway signal in the hope the driver's eyesight was excellent. He stopped, and as you settled into your seat, there was Billy Brown unsmil-ingly suggesting a pattern you should follow thereafter, "Face the driver, raise your hand. You'll find that he will understand."

The deeply placed tube lines and stations on the Underground were very popular in those disturbed times and the jam of people on the escalators was a problem. A lot of native Londoners, rather than sheepishly standing on the moving staircase, saved time by hurtling down or up, dodging the timid on the steep slope. Billy Brown was called in to sort out the speedsters and those content to rise or descend with the slow, rumbling stairs. He urged, "On the right it's stand at ease. On the left it's quick march, please."

On the tube trains, passengers peering through the skimpy triangles for a better glimpse of the stations, were inclined to pick at the edges, eventually being able to peel away some of the surrounding net covering. Billy Brown of London Town, having noted this "no-no," suddenly appeared throughout the Underground system pointing a reproving finger as he declared, "You'll pardon me for my correction. That stuff is there for your protection." Some wag promptly penned a postscript, copies of which, of course, spread like a prairie fire, "Thank you for your information — I want to see the bloody station."

It was always a comfort to be convinced one was a lot smarter than the enemy — which is why *our* discoveries were never equalled by some craven Teuton who had been submarined or parachuted onto those forever-England shores to do a spot of spying. A product of unabashed municipal pride was an age-old habit of decorating manhole covers! With all other local identification obliterated to confuse the anticipated invaders, manholes were still capped with circular cast iron covers bearing the name of the manufacturer and that of the county council customer of the firm's craftsmanship.

To my knowledge the demotion to anonymity never included manhole covers in World War II. So, when you were hopelessly lost you could be discovered, by other hopelessly lost souls and by incredulous local residents, shuffling in a circle, head down, oblivious to passing honking traffic, as you haltingly read the encircling inscription "Tees-on-Wold County Council. Albion Iron Works, Reddich Road, 1899."

So one chuckled at the erasure of Britain's face by the obliteration of signs, phone numbers, and addresses considered capable of "giving comfort to the enemy." A pox on befuddled invaders and their machinery of invasion, and on army maps "for authorized use only."

Bombers from "an airfield somewhere in Britain" were flying to an "unidentified target," allied ships were "engaging U-Boats at sea," army units were "outflanking enemy-held positions." But you, bathing in the beatific glow of rediscovery, knew exactly where you were — shuffling sideways in a happy tight circle, head down, at mid-intersection, smack-dab in the middle of Tees-On-Wold. Or were you, perhaps, on the blast furnace floor of the Albion Iron Works on Reddich Road? In any case, you knew that no longer were you lost in wartime Britain!

SUNDAY DRIVING

by Leif Montin

"You can own a car any colour you like," declared Henry Ford, "just as long as it's black." And a black Ford Model A was the first car I ever saw. I was twelve years old and had come over from Scotland only three years earlier.

The car was owned by our neighbour across the road, Dexter Smythe, who had purchased it for $549. It wouldn't have mattered to me what colour it was; it was a mysterious machine that could move at a good clip of twenty miles per hour — on a flat dry road that was well-packed. It had two forward gears and one reverse operated by a pedal on the floor.

People think that dogs chase automobiles, but in those days it was boys like myself who would run alongside, at a respectful distance, laughing and jostling for the "pole position." The dogs would chase *us*. We'd generally tire sooner than the dogs, though, and be forced out of the race while the dogs continued to bark and snap at the wheels, until they too found it futile. Then we would lean back in the shade of an old maple and watch the Model

A sputter off into the hot and dry distance, leaving only a trail of dustclouds to mark its passage on the dirt road.

Looking back, I'm sure that once boys and dogs had been left behind Smythe probably slowed to a less "breakneck" speed. After all, horses were still the most common form of transportation, and they were easily spooked by cars.

On damp days Mr. Smythe avoided trips to town, but when he did go we were treated to a real show. Although the electric starter had been invented and put to use by 1913, Ford was a big holdout against it on the grounds that economy was a more important selling feature than convenience. So on wet days Dexter Smythe would sweat away at the crank, grumbling about the miserable state of the weather in particular and the world in general. He muttered and cursed while we did our best not to smile. The only man in town with a car is not the kind of fellow a twelve-year-old wants to antagonize.

The best days, of course, were when I was the only boy around. I devotedly helped Mr. Smythe clean up the car; roads were dusty in those days, and polishing the fenders and keeping the wheels clean was almost a full-time job. After we'd given the car a spit polish, Mr. Smythe would look at me and say, "The day sure is warming up, isn't it?" This was the start of a regular game we had: would he ask me along for the ride or not?

"Well, I think I'll see about getting a little dinner right now," he'd say, while I waited for him to mention the word "ride."

Often I'd be disappointed, but hope wasn't always lost. Sometimes he would prolong my agony through the dinner hours. He probably thought it was character building.

"Yes sir," I'd say, and look across the road at my house. "I suppose I should be heading home for dinner about now too."

"When you're having dinner, why don't you ask your mother if you can come for a bit of a ride this afternoon? I'm taking a trip into town." I'd run home to wolf down a meal and present my request in pleading tones.

If I was in luck, that afternoon would find me grinning, riding high up beside Mr. Smythe.

Eight years later, automobiles were more commonplace. Trucks were numerous in the big towns and cities, where they were used for local transport. Railroads were still favoured for the long hauls. Passenger cars appeared in greater numbers too, but they were still luxury items, so parking was not exactly a big problem.

Automobiles were also better equipped by then, with many having windshield wipers, stoplights, rear-view mirrors and electric starters. By then I was driving regularly for a man named Robert Dunphy, who owned a car but would not drive it himself. He had a new Hupmobile — a beautiful car with sleek lines, but slung a little low to be really practical on unpaved roads. Roads were mostly not well-surfaced and as they were still used mostly by horse-drawn carriages, they tended to get rutted. An "improved" road was more likely than not one on which a workhorse had dragged a heavy flat board for the purpose of wearing down the hump in the middle. So driving was slow, and it required skill to negotiate country roads.

On weekends Mr. Dunphy and I would go for a drive in the countryside. Often we'd head out to a local resort town, where Alexander Graham Bell had a summer place. In fact it was the very place that Bell had experimented with his aeroplane "The Silver Dart."

Tires at that time were the tubed type, which provided a smoother ride than the old solid rubber ones, but they were also devilishly prone to punctures. In the course of a journey, it was not unusual to see three or four cars pulled over to the side of the road in trouble. And unlike today, no fellow motorist would pass a vehicle in distress without stopping to offer a helping hand.

I remember one Sunday when we made the trip without a hitch, but in town we ran into a huge pothole made by a carriage wheel. The Hupmobile, as I said, rode pretty low. After the bump it stalled and all attempts to get it started again failed miserably. Poking and prodding proved that something had shaken loose, and that the vehicle was in need of professional attention. If finding a good mechanic is difficult these days, it was utterly impossible back then.

Mr. Dunphy was starting to get tense when up from the waterside came the deep whistle of a ferry. It was as common to take the ferry in those days as it is to take an intercity bus today. The crew agreed to make room on deck for the car, and we pushed the Hupmobile on board to the sympathetic but amused looks of the crew and passengers.

In 1921, the automobile was not the fact of life it is today. It was a status symbol and a novelty. *I* didn't even buy a car until 1958, it seemed so unnecessary. Cars today have gadgets that would have been unthinkable back then. But some things never change. Cars still run out of gas on dark stretches of road when it's raining. They still grumble and splutter and stall when it's least convenient. When you think of it, a genuinely *new* mechanical problem has not been invented in a long time.

WHEN WE FIRST CAME TO THIS LAND

by Marie Barton

In Denmark, in 1910, my father worked in the brickyard by day, trundling bricks in a wheelbarrow to the kiln for baking. Then, he spent his evenings in his shop; one of the small sheds that with our slate-roofed, red-brick house formed a cobbled square. There, on his workbench, he whittled out wooden shoes for customers. Poppa had enough to do just to keep the wolves from our doorstep.

We were a large family. I was the middle child of five and it was shortly after the christening of our newest baby, Albert, that Poppa left for "America." Poppa filed a homestead of one hundred and sixty acres and prepared a home for us. At the end of that summer, he returned to ready his affairs for a permanent move to the new land.

By March of the following year, we were prepared to emigrate *en famille* to the land of opportunity. We crossed Denmark by train, the English Channel by boat, and then by train again to Liverpool to board the S.S. *Manitoba*. We sailed to St. John, N.B., and Momma was seasick during the

crossing, but my trauma began on the C.P.R. immigrant train hurtling through the rock tunnels on its way to the prairies.

The last eighteen miles from the railway station to our farm, was travelled by hired wagon and ox team. We finally arrived at our homestead on a sunny April morning, melt water lay on the land, tinted golden in the sun. The sun was reflected in the many windows in the two-room shingled house Poppa had built for us with his own hands.

I knew those windows were to help Momma see. I was only five years old but already I threaded her needles for her. I learned later that it was because of Momma's limited vision, that Grandma had consented to the marriage of her only child to Poppa, a poor man with few prospects. Grandma, a lone elderly woman left behind in Denmark, wrote often. Each time Momma read a letter from her by the light of those windows, she wept.

Poppa worked that first year for Uncle Peder, our next door neighbour, and Momma grew potatoes and turnips in the root-matted sod of her first garden.

Momma made friends with Gunda, another of our neighbours, and a fellow countrywoman from Copenhagen. "Elegant like Anna Karenina" Momma used to say of her. Gunda lived with her two young children in a homestead shack in the treeless glacial coulee below our house on the headland. Her husband, Jens Jensen, a carpenter by trade, worked long distances away building the grain elevators necessary for the ever-increasing grain yields. He only managed the long walk home once a month.

Gunda was deathly scared of the night-yodelling "wolves" (harmless prairie coyotes) that inhabited the coulee, but not so frightened of the young wolf catcher who stopped in often — presumably to taste her good Danish-brewed coffee. She taught him to speak Danish, which made it quite unnecessary for her to learn English. Poppa called her a "temptress" who should be more wary of "two-legged wolves."

Poppa was proved right when the pair eloped and Momma had to take in her two abandoned children. Often household supplies ran low.

When I was seven years old Inger, another sister, arrived during a raging snowstorm. Poppa delivered her by himself. In Denmark, he had always assisted the midwife. So then we were eight.

We were pioneers transplanted to a foreign land where we were neither literate nor articulate in the language of our new country. A very frustrating experience for any human being.

I remember that Poppa threshed his first wheat crop in 1914 by having his beasts tread "the corn" on a circular sheet of ice. The snow had come early that fall and it was impossible for a machine to move in till spring. With high hopes for the future, Poppa had disposed of his oxen that summer to move into the horse age — branded mares from the Alberta ranges, but broken to harness. The horses were tied head to tail and Poppa stood at the center and drove them round and round. He threshed three hundred bushels that way.

His ingenuity saved the day. Poppa sold some of his harvest for cash at the local elevator. He saved enough for the following spring's seed and saved a few bushels for the house. He bought a five-dollar hand mill from the T. Eaton Company for grinding wheat into whole-grain flour — a chore designated for us children.

We were a frugal family — nothing was wasted. I wore my brother's hand-me-down grain hide, leather boots with hooks (boys' shoes). My schoolmates only stopped teasing me after Momma told me to tell them to mind their own business.

My parents were very proud of their children, especially my sister Sophia. At sixteen, having worked for her room and board in town in order to go to high school, she won the Governor General's medal for obtaining the highest academic standing among three hundred grade-ten candidates in the province. Then the 1915 and '16 bumper crops sold at wartime prices enabled Poppa to help her attend the Saskatoon Normal School. A year later Sophia took charge of a one-room country school. That June she wrote her Junior Matriculation exams and passed muster.

What she could accomplish by her talents and effort, I felt I could do by sheer effort. But at fourteen, the year I graduated from grade eight at the country school, Poppa made arrangements for me to be a hired girl for a farmer's family — wages $8.00 per month; work to begin in August.

Then Mr. Harrison, my teacher on weekdays and Presbyterian lay minister on Sundays, came to my rescue. He had sent one of the stories I'd written at school to an editor of the *Playmate*, a Sunday school paper. He walked across the coulee to show it to us; my piece "The Picnic" was highlighted on the front page. Under my byline was a subheading: "by a fourteen-year-old Danish Canadian girl."

Poppa looked at Momma, and she, after having scanned it, looked at Poppa. "Gud i himmel!" (God in Heaven!) she exclaimed, "our daughter is a writer." I could see Poppa's chest swell under the bib of his striped overalls.

I was permitted to work for my board in town and go to high school — to follow in the footsteps of my brilliant sister. There was a future for us in this new land, and the future looked good.

CHAUTAUQUA REMEMBERED

by Edna S. Willoughby

Organized commercially in 1912, Chautauqua performances travelled all over the United States and many isolated parts of Canada until the early 1930s. They were conducted on a contract basis and this extremely successful cultural endeavour was welcomed in countless communities each summer — usually on a week-long run.

Although the quest for cultural benefits goes on, all the wealth of visiting artists, acoustically perfect settings, sumptuous architectural styles and decor, pales in significance when one remembers the joy with which the annual June Chautauquas were anticipated and welcomed to small towns during the early part of the century.

Among the celebrities appearing were Emmeline Pankhurst, a leader of the suffragist movement, and Vilhjalmur Steffansson, famed explorer and lecturer. Outstanding choirs, plays, orchestral groups, comics, dancers, elocutionists, and acrobats also entertained.

When the enormous khaki-coloured Chautauqua tent went up in a little town it evoked a kind of carnival spirit in young and old. Silent movies, lantern slides and periodic travelling stage companies, including the Swiss Bell Ringers, lacked the impact of a solid week of Chautauqua matinees and evening shows.

Season tickets were $3 for adults, $1.40 for students, and $1 for children. If insufficient tickets were sold, guarantors could be stuck for as much as $5 each!

Combined church services were held in the big tent on Sunday. Saturday mornings a junior Chautauqua program featured local school children who had been trained by an advance agent. To tread the stage boards under the huge, billowing canopy of canvas on those far-off mornings was pure enchantment for school kids.

Rough wooden benches provided seating on the uneven ground, from which the delicious summery smell of trampled green grass was always present. Several great support poles ran down the middle of this "big top" centre of the arts. During frequent fierce wind, thunder, hail and rain storms the big poles swayed and creaked ominously while outside guide ropes strained at perimeter stakes.

Patrons of urban centres of the arts carry quite different accessories from old-timers attending early Chautauquas. Many of the latter took along beat-up tin washtubs filled with grass to burn as smudges to ward off the hungry hordes of mosquitoes. I heard of one lady who went so far as to wind pages of newspaper under her lisle hose to combat the winged pests. Children received liberal applications of oil of citronella.

Supporters of the annual spectacle prided themselves on never missing a performance. Dreadful trips over muddy roads in buggies, democrats and balky cars were resolutely undertaken in this annual pursuit of culture. At one show patrons waded through several inches of water inside the tent after a heavy rain. Some sat perched up on the backs of seats. To save their marcelled and crimped coiffures, several ladies made and wore tams of heavy satin, which shed rain better than ordinary straw hats.

Of course all those attending were not completely culture-oriented. Some insensitive creatures, when bored, made themselves quite unpopular at times — mostly small naughty boys in the front rows who seemed unmoved by all the cultural outpourings from the stage. These lads spent many happy moments sniping at bald heads with homemade slingshots and wads of paper, or mimicking over-zealous pianists.

Chautauqua added a whole new dimension to people's lives. All the allure and delights offered by modern centres of the arts don't seem to stir up the ecstasy and wonder known during June Chautauquas. Those red-letter, community-sponsored holiday weeks left a sprinkling of cultural tidbits for young and old to mull over for a long time.

THE GREATEST SENIORS' TRIVIA QUIZ EVER!

How good is your memory? Answer the following thirty questions and find out. There are no winners or losers; this quiz is pure entertainment. Answers are provided on pages 149-150.

1. What is the boogie-woogie?
   a) a style of jazz piano
   b) a kind of dance
   c) a type of train

2. Which office building cost eighty-three million dollars to build, has seven thousand, seven hundred and forty-eight windows, and was completed in 1943?
   a) the Empire State Building
   b) the Sunlife Building
   c) the Pentagon

3. How many gold medals did Jesse Owens win in the
   1936 summer Olympic Games?
   a) six
   b) three
   c) four

4. Who was the baby in *Bringing Up Baby*?
   a) Gloria Vanderbilt
   b) a leopard
   c) Baby Jane

5. Who was the female lead in *The Gay Divorcee?*
   a) Ginger Rogers
   b) Elizabeth Taylor
   c) Zsa Zsa Gabor

6. Which product's advertising copy urged women to "Keep youth's priceless gift — that Schoolgirl Complexion"?
   a) Ivory soap
   b) Palmolive soap
   c) Pears Soap

7 In what year did Adolf Hitler become the Chancellor of Germany?
   a) 1933
   b) 1938
   c) 1930

8. Which famous British biographer and critic died in
   1932 with these last words: "If this is dying, I don't
   think much of it."
   a) George Bernard Shaw
   b) Noel Coward
   c) Giles Lytton Strachey

9. Who sang "There'll be Bluebirds Over the White
   Cliffs of Dover"?
   a) Vera Lynn
   b) Dinah Shore
   c) Judy Garland

10. Which film won eleven Academy Awards in 1959?
    a) *Gone with the Wind*
    b) *Ben Hur*
    c) *Bedtime for Bonzo*

11. Which 1943 musical extravaganza featured an all-black cast that included Lena Horne, Cab Calloway, Fats Waller and the Nicholas Brothers?
   a) *Ain't Misbehavin'*
   b) *Stormy Weather*
   c) *Showboat*

12. In which Marx Brothers' film did Groucho and Chico negotiate a contract where the insanity clause was removed because Chico claimed "You can't fool me. There ain't no sanity clause."?
   a) *A Day at the Races*
   b) *Duck Soup*
   c) *A Night at the Opera*

13. Harry James was famous for playing:
   a) the trumpet
   b) the fool
   c) the tables

14. Identify the man convicted of kidnapping the Lindbergh baby in 1932.
   a) Albert DeSalvo
   b) Bruno Richard Hauptmann
   c) Frank Nitty

15. Who or what was Morocco bound?
   a) Webster's Dictionary
   b) German Tank Commander General Rommel
   c) Hope and Crosby
   d) all of the above

16. Which baseball outfielder hit
seven hundred and fourteen
home runs in twenty-two
seasons?
   a) Ty Cobb
   b) Babe Ruth
   c) Honus Wagner

17. Who wrote *An American in
Paris*?
   a) George Gershwin
   b) General Eisenhower
   c) Ernest Hemingway

18. Mae West had some fabulous one-liners in her films, but one of the following statements attributed to her is incorrect. Which is it?
    a) "It's better to be looked over than to be overlooked."
    b) "Why don't you come up and see me sometime?"
    c) "When women go wrong, men go right after them."

19. Besides claiming that they "put the *moo* in *smooth*," which company in the '40s claimed "If it's **** it's got to be good."
    a) Gordon's (Ice Cream Co.)
    b) Borden's (Milk Co.)
    c) Sealtest (Dairy)

20. Which baseball player was famous for his hook slide?
    a) Lou Gehrig
    b) Joe DiMaggio
    c) Pee Wee Reese

21. What does HMV stand for?
    a) Home Movie Viewer
    b) Her Majesty's Vanguard
    c) His Master's Voice

22. Identify the actor and actress who starred in *The Thin Man* film series.
    a) George Powell and Carole Lombard
    b) William Powell and Myrna Loy
    c) Clark Gable and Claudette Colbert

23. What song was the orchestra playing as the great ship *Titanic* went down?
    a) "Ave Maria"
    b) "Nearer My God to Thee"
    c) "Ragtime"

24. In the film *Swiss Miss*, which famous comedic duo yodelled their way through the Swiss Alps?
    a) Hope and Crosby
    b) Laurel and Hardy
    c) Abbott and Costello

25. What was the number one record
    listed on Billboard's chart in the
    issue of July 20th, 1940?
    a) "I'll Never Smile Again" by
       Tommy Dorsey
    b) "Let's Dance" by Benny
       Goodman
    c) "Stardust" by Artie Shaw

26. Whose first commercial recording
    was the song "I've Got the Girl" in
    1926?
    a) Al Jolson
    b) Bing Crosby
    c) Eddie Cantor

27. What fashion trend did performer
    Colleen Moore make popular during
    the flapper era?
    a) fringed dresses
    b) short haircuts
    c) feathered eyelashes

28.When you danced to the big bands of the '30s,
which of the following dances were you most likely
to be doing?
a) the Peabody, the Black Bottom, the Fox Trot
b) the Shake, the Limbo, the Boogaloo
c) the Shag, the Shuffle-Shag, the Jitterbug

29.Who is considered the fastest talker in public life so
far this century?
a) Al Capone
b) John F. Kennedy
c) Monty Hall

30.How old was Satchel Paige when he was finally admitted to the major leagues?
a) thirty-six years old
b) forty-two years old
c) too old to play ball

ANSWERS

1. a) This style of piano playing was especially popular in the '30s. Great to dance to!
2. c) It also covers more ground area than any other office building in the world.
3. c) He won the gold medals in the one hundred and two hundred meter dash, the four hundred meter relay, and the broad jump.
4. b) It starred with Cary Grant and Katherine Hepburn in this hilarious comedy.
5. a) — in the movie version, but in real life b) and c) are neck and neck.
6. b) The famed "Palmolive Girl" played golf and tennis, rode a horse, and travelled in the desert on the '20s billboard advertisements for "The Palm and Olive Oil Soap."
7. a) — and between that year and 1941 he conquered more of Europe than Napoleon ever did.
8. c) A member of The Bloomsbury Group, he was admired for his wit and style.
9. a) She was Britain's most famous songstress during WWII.
10. b) This extravaganza was the only eleven-Oscar winner in Academy history.
11. b) But "Ain't Misbehavin' " is part of the original score.
12. c) By the by, do you remember which opera they were putting on? It was Verdi's *Il Travatore*.
13. a) — although he was sometimes known to play b), and was rumoured to play c).
14. b) — although he went to the electric chair declaring his innocence.
15. d) Bing and Bob were always on the road to somewhere, but even the dictionary was bound in Moroccan leather.
16. b) This talented man was also a first rate pitcher too.
17. a) — although Eisenhower and Hemingway spent considerable time there.
18. b) What she said was, "Come up and see me some time." Mae West never asked, she commanded.
19. b) This company's 1940s billboard featured Elsie the Cow.
20. b) Mind you, the other two weren't exactly chopped liver.

21. c) His Master's Voice Gramophone Company, whose famous logo featured a wind-up gramophone and a dog.
22. b) Powell and Loy.
23. b) It was the last song ever heard by the one thousand, five hundred people who went down with the ship.
24. b) This was a variety show kind of film, set in the Tyrol.
25. a) — but Dorsey must have smiled all the way to his bank.
26. b) And he was relatively unknown at the time.
27. b) No one is quite sure who popularized the other two.
28. c) Remember doing these to Glen Miller? You would have danced group a) to Jack Teagarden in the '20s.
29. b) He was once clocked at three hundred and twenty-seven words per minute.
30. b) It took him forty-two years to break the colour barrier.